Contents

- **3** Editorial: Grace in Pandemic Proportions
- **7** *Craig S. Keener*
  Jesus and Would-be Disciples
- **11** *Marie McInnes*
  Abraham and Moses in the Gospels
- **24** *Michael J. Kok*
  Re-naming the Toll Collector in Matthew 9:9: A review of the options
- **35** *Peter G. Bolt*
  A Certain Wisdom in Nazareth (Mark 6:2b)
- **50** *Craig A. Evans*
  Jesus and Asclepius in the Gospel of John
- **69** *Christoph Stenschke*
  "When they heard this, they were silenced" (Acts 11:18): Some Inner-Christian Conflicts and Their Resolution in Acts 6–15:35

Book Reviews

- **90** Darrell L. Bock, *Jesus, Skepticism & The Problem of History: A Book Report and Some Core Issues* (HarperCollins Religious - US, 2019)
- **96** Seán Freyne, *The Jesus Movement and Its Expansion: Meaning and Mission* (Grand Rapids & Cambridge, UK: Eerdmans, 2014)
- **99** Tom Thatcher, Chris Keith, Raymond F. Person, Jr., and Elsie R. Stern (eds.), *The Dictionary of the Bible and Ancient Media* (London: T&T Clark, 2017)
- **101** Jeannine Brown, *The Gospels as Stories: A Narrative Approach to Matthew, Mark, Luke and John* (Grand Rapids: Baker Academic, 2020)
- **103** Sarah Harris, *The Davidic Shepherd King in the Lucan Narrative* (LNTS 558. London: T & T Clark, 2016)
- **105** Ray Clendenen, *Jesus' Opening Week: A Deep Exegesis of John 1:1–2:11* (Eugene: Wipf & Stock, 2019)
- **107** Jörg Frey, *The Glory of the Crucified One: Christology and Theology in the Gospel of John* (Waco, TX: Baylor University Press, 2018)
- **110** John Behr, *John the Theologian and his Paschal Gospel: A Prologue to Theology* (Oxford: OUP, 2019)
- **113** Andrew W. Pitts, *History, Biography, and the Genre of Luke-Acts: An Exploration of Literary Divergence in Greek Narrative Discourse* (Leiden and Boston: Brill, 2019)

Grace in Pandemic Proportions

An editorial cannot be written in 2020 without reference to the global COVID-19 pandemic that has shut down the world and is still in progress as *JGAR* volume 4 is published. As I write, the official numbers show that there have been 31.4 million cases worldwide, with 21.5 million already recovered. Tragically, however, 967,000 people have lost their lives to this disease that still awaits an effective vaccine. In the last global pandemic exactly 100 years ago, an estimated 500 million people became infected with 'Spanish Flu' (H1N1 virus) with at least 50 million losing their lives.[1] We should all be praying that in God's grace it will get better before it becomes worse.

At this stage, how can we even quantify the effects on societies, families, and individuals as a result of the virus and its consequences—the shutdowns, the shrinking economies, the loss of work, the effects on educational institutions, etc, etc, etc.—let alone evaluate the significance of this disaster for the future? The rhetoric of 'the old normal' and 'the new normal' has already become part of the common conversation, even if we cannot yet see what that new normal might bring. We should all be praying that in God's grace it will be better rather than worse.

Amongst the many effects and the massive shutdowns, the *Centre for Gospels and Acts Research*, cancelled a planned Colloquium on Genre in April, joined the multitude of online-only meetings for the rest of this year, and is already planning that the Centre's conference in one year's time may still need to allow for online presentation and attendance in order to maximise the necessary social distancing that may assist, and minimise the face-to-face mingling that may inhibit, humanity's survival of this crisis that is concrete and real.

We are used to 'crises' that are declared merely as part of the rhetoric and propaganda of a particular interest-group in order to create the fear that is thought necessary to motivate human beings to change, or to join a particular cause for the betterment of society and the world. Sadly, even as the world struggles to survive what is a real crisis at last, there have been those who

---

1 www.cdc.gov/flu/pandemic-resources/1918-pandemic-h1n1.html.

EDITORIAL GRACE IN PANDEMIC PROPORTIONS

declare it nothing in proportion to the crises of their own inventions. Even at a time when all should, and so many are, pulling together in common human cause, others wish to keep the rhetoric of conflict and division rolling on as part of competing political agendas. But nothing new emerges without some kind of conflict with the old.

As Jesus of Nazareth commenced his ministry in Galilee he announced a crisis that he labelled 'good news' for the world. The times are fulfilled. The kingdom of God has drawn near. The Gospels and Acts report on that crisis and how the message that flowed out of it was reported to 'turn the world upside down' (Acts 17:6). The detractors of the earliest Jesus movement saw that as a bad thing. Its supporters saw it as good. But both agreed that this movement was significantly changing the world as it once was known. There was an old normal that was becoming increasingly nervous as this rapidly spreading movement was urging others to enter a new normal. Whether the call for a new normal was good or bad, depended upon a person's position in relation to this new movement. The eschatological clash between the kingdoms of this world and the kingdom of God, expected by the apocalyptic types, had now begun.

The Gospel and Acts report on those times, for the sake of all times. And for us who live in these times. The 21st century world presents opportunities and challenges that require the message about Jesus Christ to be continually re-presented with clarity and concern. That won't be without debate and discussion, and it won't be without the call for the old to give way to the new. Such clarification and concern requires serious and careful research into the foundation documents of the Christian movement.

The theme of the Centre for Gospels and Acts Research 2021 conference (Sept 20 & Oct 1) is:

Jesus: Beginning, Middle, and End of Time?
Eschatology in Gospels and Acts Research

Although he will no longer have the joy (or trouble!) of travelling to Australia, Professor Craig Evans, John Bisagno Distinguished Professor of Christian Origins at Houston Baptist University, will bring two keynote addresses to the conference, under the theme of *Kingdoms in Conflict: The Jesus Movement and the Roman Empire*. Two of our own scholars, Associate Professor Michele Connolly and Dr Debra Snoddy will also deliver keynotes—one from Mark, the other from John. Other papers have been called for. Provoked by the present need for social distancing that may well continue into next year, presenters and delegates will be able to participate in the conference remotely through the online facilities that have so quickly become part of our daily lives. As the old wineskins must be left aside, the new wineskins bring with them unforeseen advantages: those who might otherwise have been inhibited by distance from attending can now participate.

Perhaps it is this clash of the new with the old that helps to tie the articles in this fourth issue of the *Journal of Gospels and Acts Research* together. Even ahead of his address at next year's conference, Craig Evans already delves into the 'kingdoms in conflict' theme, as he looks at the ancient perception of the rivalry between Jesus and the healing god Asclepius, and how the Gospel of John enters into that debate. Whereas the new Christian movement may have found itself in conflict with the religious movements of the ancient world, Christoph Stenschke seeks to understand how it dealt with conflicts that arose from within its own ranks, according to the book of Acts, and how these conflicts were brought to resolution even as the new movement continued to emerge. Marie McInnes examines the role of Abraham and Moses in the four Gospels, especially in relation to the polemics involved in the self-definition of earliest Christianity over against Judaism. Craig Keener situates Jesus' call for others to follow him in the context of similar calls from Jewish rabbis and Greek teachers, noting Jesus' demands for true disciples to walk on a narrow way that sets them apart from their world. Michael Kok turns to Matthew's account of one particular man who was called to follow Jesus, who was given the label of 'tax-collector', when this profession was regarded as inimical to the teaching of the new way. My own essay suggests that the synagogue of Nazareth asked a nuanced question about Jesus' wisdom and powers in order to put a distance between themselves and their favourite son, becoming an example of resistance to his call in favour of the status quo. The choice of the old over against the new.

The more things change, perhaps the more things stay the same. Perhaps the more things stay the same, the less we see the need for lasting change. Perhaps the more things are shaken by a world crisis, the more we are challenged to be like that householder who brings out of his storeroom treasures both old and new (Matt 13:52). Perhaps a crisis of pandemic proportions will open the storehouses of God's grace in a magnitude of as yet unseen proportions.

Peter G. Bolt
Executive Editor

Jesus and Would-be Disciples

CRAIG S. KEENER

Abstract

Did Jesus always choose his disciples, rather than have the disciples choose him, as in Rabbinic tradition? Just as with Jewish rabbis and Greek wise men, prospective disciples also approached Jesus, but his heavy demands on their life turned them away. His goal was not to turn them away, but to make them sufficiently count the cost in order to become true disciples.

Key Words: rabbinic disciples; Jesus' disciples; cost of discipleship; Diogenes; Zeno.

It has often been argued that the manner in which Jesus chose his disciples was unusual—indeed, that disciples normally chose their Rabbis rather than the reverse.[1] This contention seems to be at least partly right; the bulk of our available evidence does in fact suggest that disciples normally sought their own teachers. But the assertion that Jesus expressed his authority by choosing disciples is not nuanced enough, since prospective disciples did approach Jesus. Jesus sometimes thrust them aside,[2] but this thrusting aside of prospective disciples was not at all unheard of in antiquity, and indeed often served only to test the would-be student's real willingness to become a learner.

The Cost of Rabbinic Discipleship

Despite the relative lateness of our rabbinic sources on the subject, it would be unlikely that they would not reflect *any* measure of historical tradition. As we shall see, the rabbinic model of discipleship also has Greek parallels which are no doubt free from Jewish and Christian influence and which probably indicate some pre-Christian patterns of discipleship.

Although disciples of Rabbis normally remained with their wives during study, at least by the time of our second century sources, there are indications that this was not always the case.[3] An epideictic story about Rabbi Akiba, whether wholly or only partly apocryphal, reflects the views of this period: having returned home after years of study, he heard that his wife was willing to be apart from him for as many more years, for the

---

1   E.g., Gundry, *Matthew*, 62. Malina, *The NT World*, 78, gives this suggestion a new twist: Jesus calling the disciples represents a diminution of his own status to initiate 'bonds or alliances with others', so that Jesus' act here is not one of authority but one of humble service.

2   As Shammai, schematically contrasted with the gentle Hillel in Rabbinic tradition, is said to have done with prospective converts.

3   Cf. Safrai, 'Education and the Study of the Torah', 965.

sake of his learning—whereupon he returned to his studies and came back to her at their completion with an abundance of disciples.[4] Similarly,[5] R. Simeon ben Yohai and another Rabbi were said to have left their families for thirteen years to study under Akiba.[6] While these seem to be patent exaggerations—Tannaitic teaching forbids leaving one's wife for more than thirty days to engage in Torah study[7]—they may indicate that despite rulings of first-century schools prohibiting long-term abstinence, some Jewish men would go to study with famous teachers of the Law.[8] It is at least clear that those who circulated these traditions about Akiba and his disciples viewed such sacrifice as laudatory regardless of the Rabbinic rulings on separation from one's spouse.

Disciples Approaching Teachers

The Mishnah contends that it is the disciple's responsibility to procure a teacher for himself. Joshua ben Perachiah, a pre-Christian sage, reportedly advised this, as well as acquiring a חָבֵר, a companion (presumably for Torah study).[9] Rabban Gamaliel repeated the same advice in another context.[10] Likewise, a writer for Socrates in the Cynic Epistles advises choosing a good education and a wise teacher.[11]

But not all teachers were willing to accept prospective disciples. This is particularly true in the Cynic and Stoic traditions. It is said that Diogenes persisted in following Antisthenes despite the latter's attempts to drive him (and others) away.[12] Diogenes apparently came to regard this as a useful pedagogical technique for his own would-be disciples: 'Someone wanted to study philosophy under him. Diogenes gave him a tunny to carry and told him to follow him. And when for shame the man threw it away and departed, some time after on meeting him he laughed and said, "The friendship between you and me was broken by a tunny"'.[13]

Nor was Diogenes alone, according to Diogenes Laertius, our main source for this tradition. Similar stories are told of the early Stoic Zeno. In a story that reminds us of Jesus' confrontation with the rich young ruler, it is said that: 'A Rhodian, who was handsome and rich, but nothing more, insisted on joining his class; but so unwelcome was this pupil, that first of all Zeno made him sit on the benches that were dusty, that he might soil his cloak, and then he consigned him to the place where the beggars sat, that he might rub shoulders with their rags; so at last the young man went away'.[14]

But what is probably more significant is the implication that such teachers allowed those who persisted to actually become their disciples, as in the case of a wealthy young man Diogenes despised. As the story goes, the young man, impressed, distributed all

---

4   Sandmel, *Judaism and Christian Beginnings*, 246–47, citing b. Ned. 50a; cf. Witherington, *Women in the Ministry of Jesus*, 10, citing b. Ket. 62b–63a. On the enormous number of disciples (and explanations how they all died off), see b. Yeb. 62b; Gen. Rab. 61:3; Eccl. Rab. 11:6, §1.
5   This story, of course, could be a transferral of the Akiba story to these others.
6   Gen. Rab. 95 (MSV).
7   M. Ket. 13:10, 5:6, cited in Safrai, 'Home and Family', 763. It is not clear that all Jewish teachers in the first century would have felt obligated to follow the rulings of the schools, but by the period of Akiba and his disciples, this would be a standard ruling followed by all in the Rabbinic movement, unless exceptions could be made for Torah study.
8   Although the condition of spouses is not mentioned, stories like that of Hillel, a Babylonian immigrant, nearly freezing to death sitting in the window to hear Shemaiah and Abtalion may reflect such a practice.
9   M. Abot 1:6.
10 M. Abot 1:16. Both sayings are very concisely formulated and probably reflect the same editing.
11 Socrates 4 (tr. S. K. Stowers), in Malherbe, *The Cynic Epistles*, 228–29.
12 Diogenes Laertius, *Lives* 6.2.21.
13 Diogenes Laertius, *Lives* 6.2.36; he also cites a variant version, just as useful for our point, as reported by Diocles.
14 Diogenes Laertius, *Lives* 7.1.22 (Loeb 2:132–33).

his property and adopted the Cynic lifestyle.[15] Diogenes also actively 'persuaded Crates to give up his fields…, and throw into the sea any money he had'.[16]

Diogenes was actually willing to attract disciples—provided they were willing to pay the appropriate price for following him. Onesicritus of Aegina 'is said to have sent to Athens the one of his two sons named Androsthenes, and he having become a pupil of Diogenes stayed there; the father then sent the other also, the aforesaid Philiscus, who was the elder, in search of him; but Philiscus was also detained in the same way. When, thirdly, the father himself arrived, he was just as much attracted to the pursuit of philosophy as his sons and joined the circle—so magical was the spell which the discourses of Diogenes exerted'.[17]

We may compare this to Jesus' demand that disciples be willing to forsake even familial obligations to follow his teaching.[18] All of this fits Martin Hengel's proposal that Jesus's calling of disciples follows the model of a charismatic leader (even if we have to broaden our definition of charismatic here) rather than that of institutional teachers like the later Rabbis.[19]

Conclusion

Although Jesus may have gone beyond many of the Rabbis in seeking out disciples, he also turned away prospective disciples with heavy demands. But it is not unlikely that his intentions were similar to those of Greek teachers who had observed the same practice: to force disciples to count the cost, to stop relying on their prior assets, and to recognize the true value of the teaching.

The anticipated response, then, is the same sort of response offered by persistent seekers throughout the Jesus tradition: the Syrophoenician woman (Mark 7:27–29), blind Bartimaeus (Mark 10:48–52), the Gentile centurion (Matt. 8:7–13[20]), and the mother of Jesus (John 2:3–9).[21] Many studies[22] have documented the *chutspah*, the holy boldness, of charismatic teachers; but teachers like Jesus apparently demanded the same sort of boldness from those who would learn their way of life. Jesus' sorrow over the unwilling disciple (Mark 10:23–25) indicates that his goal was not to turn disciples away, but rather to make them become true disciples, which they could only do by counting the cost and choosing the narrow way of following him.

---

15 Diogenes 38 (tr. Benjamin Fiore), in Malherbe, *Cynic Epistles*, 162–63. The Rabbis more frequently tell such stories with regard to conversion to Judaism (e.g., Sipre Num. 115.5.7), which more strictly parallels philosophical conversion than adopting a Jewish teacher would have.
16 Diogenes Laertius, *Lives* 6.5.87, citing Diocles (Loeb 2:90–91).
17 Diogenes Laertius, *Lives* 6.2.75–76 (Loeb 2:76–79). Cf. 1 Samuel 19 for an Israelite example of a similar phenomenon with regard to the Spirit of prophecy.
18 Matthew 8; Luke 9 (with its added Elijah-Elisha parallel).
19 See Hengel, *The Charismatic Leader*, 1–2, 27–33.
20 Especially if verse 7 is construed as a question.
21 It is also found in earlier Jewish tradition, e.g., 2 Kings 4:28.
22 E.g., Vermes, *Jesus the Jew*, 79–80.

Bibliography

Gundry, Robert H.	*Matthew: A Commentary on his Literary and Theological Art* (Grand Rapids: Eerdmans, 1982).
Hengel, Martin	*The Charismatic Leader and his Followers* (John Riches, ed.; James Greig, tr.; New York: Crossroad, 1981).
Malherbe, A. J. (ed.)	*The Cynic Epistles: A Study Edition* (SBLSBS 12; Missoula: SBL, 1977).
Malina, Bruce J.	*The NT World: Insights from Cultural Anthropology* (Atlanta: John Knox, 1981).
Safrai, S.	'Home and Family', in S. Safrai & M. Stern, with D. Flusser & W. C. van Unnik (eds.), *The Jewish People in the First Century* (2 vols.; Assen & Philadelphia: Van Gorcum, 1974–1976), 728–92.
Safrai, S.	'Education and the Study of the Torah', in S. Safrai & M. Stern, with D. Flusser & W. C. van Unnik (eds.), *The Jewish People in the First Century* (2 vols.; Assen & Philadelphia: Van Gorcum, 1974–1976), 945–70.
Sandmel, Samuel	Judaism and Christian Beginnings (New York: Oxford University Press, 1978).
Vermes, Geza	*Jesus the Jew: A Historian's Reading of the Gospels* (Philadelphia: Fortress, 1973).
Witherington, Ben, III	*Women in the Ministry of Jesus* (SNTSM 51; Cambridge: Cambridge University Press, 1984).

Abraham and Moses in the Gospels

MARIE MCINNES

Abstract

Abraham and Moses are frequently mentioned in all four Gospels. The roles of each figure are broadly twofold: Abraham is a covenant partner and the universal father; Moses is the Lawgiver and the Leader-cum-Prophet. Although the fatherhood of Abraham is always regarded approvingly, it is often used negatively against perceived enemies, especially in John. Moses as Lawgiver is not only used negatively against the Pharisees, but is also regarded rather unfavourably in Matthew and John. John's Gospel, in particular, downplays Moses in his roles as Lawgiver (in relation to circumcision) and as Leader (regarding the gift of manna). From Mark to Luke to Matthew to John, there is an intensification of polemic against Abraham's false sons and against Moses' false disciples. But there is also a rise in polemic against Moses himself, reaching a peak in John.

Key Words: Gospels, Abraham, Moses, John the Baptist, Pharisees, Law, Gentiles

Abraham and Moses, along with David, are the Old Testament characters most frequently mentioned in the Gospels and Acts.[1] They each have two predominant roles in the Gospels which are analysed, first in the Synoptics and in John; the passages in which they appear together are then considered. Finally, possible connections and contrasts between the two figures and their various roles are explored, with consideration of the way in which they are both regarded and used across the Gospels, with a glance at Acts and the Pauline epistles.

1. Abraham

There are numerous Gospel passages where the name of Abraham occurs: the bulk of references belong to the Gospels of Matthew and Luke combined, although the writers often have different perspectives. John has multiple references to Abraham in one lengthy and complex discourse (ch. 8) and Mark has a sole reference which he shares with the other Synoptics. The function of Abraham is broadly twofold: 1) as a party to covenantal promises, sometimes with Isaac and

---

[1] Noah, Jonah, Elijah and the writing prophets, Isaiah and Jeremiah, are also mentioned but not as frequently. Elijah will be considered briefly regarding his role with Moses on the Mount of Transfiguration. I will not consider Acts except in passing, as most of its references are found in straightforward salvation history narratives.

Jacob, within salvation history; 2) as the exemplar of universal fatherhood. The second role is far more important in the Gospels. Several passages contain more than one category; the extended disputation between Jesus and his listeners in John 8, for example, covers both.

1.1 A Covenant Partner

Abraham's roles as covenant partner and universal father are closely linked. There is a difference, however, in that the fatherhood of Abraham is often used negatively against perceived enemies whereas the covenantal aspect of salvation history is invariably positive.

1.1.1 The Synoptics

The contrast between the genealogies in Matthew and Luke lies in the differing aims of the two evangelists. If Matthew's aim is to prove that Jesus is the Messiah and the fulfilment of Old Testament prophecy, this can explain why he begins his Gospel with Jesus' descent from Abraham: the promise that all nations would be blessed by him (Gen 17:5) was the beginning of salvation history. Matthew highlights Jesus' messianic credentials but also his place in the royal-messianic line, hence his privileging also of the descent from David. It is noteworthy that Matthew mentions both Abraham and David in the first sentence of his Gospel, juxtaposing both the Abrahamic and Davidic covenants which, unlike the Sinaitic covenant, are universal and unconditional. If, on the other hand, biological descent is of lesser importance to Luke, this explains why he places his genealogy at the start of Jesus' ministry (3:23). He traces Jesus' ancestry in the opposite direction and ends with Adam, the son of God.[2] His concern with humanity as a whole rather than Jewish ancestry is manifest in many later references to Abraham, and in his Gospel as a whole.

The frequent mention of Abraham, along with Jacob/Israel, contributes to the strong Semitic flavour of Luke's Canticles. Mary's invocation of the one 'who spoke to our fathers, to Abraham and his posterity for ever' (1:55) includes Abraham among the fathers in contrast to Zechariah who refers to Abraham alone: 'the oath which the Lord God of Israel swore to our father Abraham' (1:73). While Mary is concerned with mercy, Zechariah dwells on the promise of deliverance from enemies. Mary mentions both the 'house of Jacob' and 'Israel', a reference to the nation. Neither canticle is particularly concerned with the universal nature of the Incarnation; rather, the growing expectation of national-political developments in the Second Temple period is clear.[3] Whenever the promises are mentioned in the Canticles, they are seen in the context of the Abrahamic covenant (Mary in 1:55 and Zechariah, in 1:73) or the Davidic (Zechariah in 1:69) but not the Mosaic.

1.1.2 The Gospel of John

Only one allusion to Abraham in John can be construed as pertaining to salvation history.

In 8:56, after a discussion about Abraham as the archetypal father (which will be discussed below), Jesus makes the astounding claim: 'Abraham rejoiced to see my day...'. The verb ἠγαλλιάσατο may refer to Gen 17:17, taking Abraham's laughter, as the rabbis did, as a sign of joy at the birth of Isaac who might be seen as the first instalment of the promises which God made to his father.[4]

---

2 This is intended to stress the divine origin of the human race. Luke suggests, as Paul makes explicit in Rom. 5, that Jesus is the new Adam. There is perhaps a link with Paul's reference to God's offspring in Acts 17:28.
3 Hagner, *How New is the New Testament?*, 37.
4 Vawter, 'The Gospel according to John', 443.

It is more likely that the meaning is that Abraham knew that the promises pointed to a future blessedness, which was to be realised in the Messiah.[5]

1.2 Exemplar of Fatherhood

Abraham is most often held up in the Gospels as the touchstone of fatherhood and, by extension, sonship. In episodes which centre on John the Baptiser, the Roman centurion, and Zacchaeus, Abraham is invoked as 'father' both by those who follow Jesus and those who oppose him. Among the Synoptics, there is more breadth in Luke's treatment of fatherhood in John the Baptiser's address at the Jordan with the inclusion of various classes of society. In John 8 Jesus enunciates an even higher view of Abrahamic descent than does John the Baptiser in Matthew, along with the most scathing critique of those who falsely claim to be Abraham's sons.

1.2.1 Abraham as Father: The Synoptics

John the Baptiser uses Abraham to castigate those who came to him to be baptised; both Matthew (3:7–12) and Luke (3:7–14) record the encounter in which John tells his audience that they cannot trust in their physical descent from Abraham. For Luke's Baptiser, the 'sons of Abraham' demonstrate their family resemblance to Abraham through their behaviour in the sphere of socioeconomic relationships.[6] Matthew mentions Pharisees and Sadduccees, which is strange since they were bitter enemies, whereas Luke has ὄχλοι (3:7); it is rather surprising that he describes them as γεννήματα ἐχιδνῶν. Luke is consistent, however, in that tax-gatherers and soldiers seek advice from John (Luke 3:10–14). If Matthew is later than Luke and is less directly connected with eyewitness sources, as Bauckham believes,[7] perhaps we can surmise that his anti-Pharisaism is due to a hardening of divisions in the interim.[8]

Luke alone singles out two outsiders for the epithet 'daughter/son of Abraham': the crippled woman who desires to be set free from a disabling spirit on the Sabbath (13:16), and Zacchaeus the tax-gatherer who shows his repentance (19:9). Luke's aim, in the latter case, is to challenge the prejudices of his day by calling the traitorous, greedy, diminutive outcast 'a son of Abraham'.[9] By including a woman long bound by Satan and a hated man in the Abrahamic family, Luke signals the universality of Jesus' ministry.

Abraham, along with Isaac and Jacob, is mentioned in Matthew and Luke in the description of 'the Messianic Banquet'. Here Abraham, Isaac and Jacob might be seen as the recipients of the covenant promises; Luke adds 'and the prophets', perhaps an allusion to messianic prophecy throughout the Old Testament. The pericope is found in very different contexts, in line with the varying preoccupations of the evangelists. In Matthew, Jesus commends the faith of the centurion

---

5   The reference reads as more than prophetic insight; one wonders if Jesus is alluding to an encounter with the angel of the covenant, as recorded in Genesis 17. A parallel is made later in the Gospel, not by Jesus but the evangelist himself: in an editorial aside in 12:41 John claims that Isaiah saw Christ's glory and spoke of him, a reference to Isaiah 6.
6   Green, *Conversion in Luke-Acts*, 118.
7   Bauckham, 'Fourteen Years Later', 14. A comparison between the Sermon on the Mount and the Sermon on the Plain provides evidence for Luke's priority: it seems more likely that Matthew collates Luke's sayings into a coherent whole than that Luke dispersed Matthew's around his Gospel, sometimes without much context.
8   In John, the Baptiser is seen totally within his own community of followers; he points them to Jesus while debasing himself in comparison.
9   Parsons, '"Short in Stature"', 55. It could also be argued that Zacchaeus is Abrahamic in his intention to make restitution; restitution equals hospitality for which Abraham is famous, based on Abraham's action in Gen 18:1–8, referred to in Heb 13:2 (Green, *Conversion*, 18).

whose servant is at death's door and concludes: 'Many will come from east and west,[10] and recline at table with Abraham, Isaac and Jacob in the kingdom of heaven' (8:11). The 'table' is often seen as a reference to Isa 25:6,[11] a festive banquet which the Lord of hosts prepares on Mount Zion. But here the three patriarchs of Genesis, rather than the Messiah, host the meal. Jesus goes on to say that '*the sons of the kingdom* will be thrown into the outer darkness; in that place there will be weeping and gnashing of teeth' (8:12). It is not clear what Jesus means by οἱ υἱοὶ τῆς βασιλείας— perhaps it is ironic. If Matthew was written first, Luke may have omitted the phrase because he did not understand it; if Luke is first, Matthew perhaps moved the scene to make a contrast between nominal sons and real sons. The kingdom to which Matthew's sons belong cannot be identified with the sons of the kingdom in the Parable of the Weeds (Matt 13:3), since they are the good seed. A clue may be found in the Parable of the Vineyard where Jesus concludes: 'The kingdom of God will be taken away from you and given to a nation producing fruit' (Matt 21:43); therefore they are disinherited sons. The contrast with the 'many that shall come from east and west' is not as stark as the stones from which, John the Baptiser claims, God can raise up sons (Matt 3:9; Luke 3:8) but it makes the same point: the ones who falsely rely on sonship are the farthest away from it.

In Luke's version (13:28–30) the idea of disinherited sons is missing; he moves the messianic banquet to another context, during Jesus' peripatetic ministry around towns and villages (13:22), linking it with Matthew's saying in the Sermon on the Mount: 'Not everyone who says Lord, Lord...' (7:21). Luke does not make clear whether Jesus is addressing his hearers directly or continuing a more general diatribe against those who falsely claim affinity. Luke's account begins negatively (with the weeping and gnashing of teeth) but ends positively with the guests at the banquet; Matthew's is the reverse. Matthew thus accentuates the unbelief of those claiming descent from Abraham while Luke focuses on their actions.

The parable, or more correctly allegory, of Dives and Lazarus (Luke 16:19–31)[12] portrays Abraham as warden of Paradise and as the comforter of those who had been oppressed in this life. It is akin to the role that Abraham, Isaac and Jacob are given at the messianic banquet but the use of the phrase εἰς τὸν κόλπον Ἀβραάμ is more informal and fatherly. This is reinforced by the fact that Dives three times addresses Abraham as 'Father' and in return Abraham calls the rich man 'son' but only once. Abraham is decidedly not the historical character known from Genesis; his name is borrowed from the trope of 'Abraham's bosom'. The Messianic feast, the reward which is denied to Dives, is similar to that mentioned in connection with the Messianic banquet, in that Lazarus is taken by angels and is seen in a position of honour. Good life leads to evil afterlife while the reverse is true for Lazarus, based on the common Jewish assumption that the next world exists to put right the injustices of this world.[13] For that reason, Abraham exercises his power to refuse entry to Dives.

---

10 The coming from east and west is usually thought to refer to the influx of the Gentiles but some critics see it as the ingathering of the Diaspora; the east and west denote Egypt and Assyria/Babylon. But Jesus is never depicted as reflecting on the Diaspora and, moreover, the journey of the Magi, peculiar to Matthew, was a harbinger of the coming of Gentiles prophesied in Isa 2:2. Furthermore, the Great Commission mentions 'all nations' (Matt 28:19).
11 'On this mountain the Lord of hosts will make for all peoples a feast of rich food...' A similar banquet is mentioned in the Dead Sea Scrolls: 'When the Messiah comes the chiefs of the clans of Israel shall gather at the common table to eat and drink new wine' (1QSª, in Vermes, *The Complete Dead Sea Scrolls*, 159–60).
12 Along with the parable of the Great Assize (Matt 25:31–46), the material is drawn not from everyday life but the imagery of late Jewish apocalyptic, which would have been familiar to the hearers (Barth, *CD*, 4.3.1, p. 19).
13 Bauckham, 'The Rich Man and Lazarus', 232.

1.2.2 Abraham as Father in John

The greatest cluster of allusions to Abraham as ancestral father is found in Jesus' disputation with the unbelieving Jews in John 8, around the Feast of Tabernacles. The recurrence of the name 'Abraham' seems to give the passage a sense of unity, but there are shifts in logic which are not easy to follow. The pivot on which the conversation turns is the concept of freedom. Jesus' interlocutors (initially called Pharisees and later οἱ Ιουδαῖοι) naively believe that their freedom consists in being Abraham's children because they have the Word contained in the Law. They are unable to see that they are not free, because they seem to take Jesus literally: according to the Torah, no Israelite was ever to be treated as a slave (Lev 25:39–53); Jesus, however, seems to be speaking of a spiritual slavery to sin. At one point he concedes the Jews' claim: 'I know that you are Abraham's seed' (v. 37), the use of the word σπέρμα indicating a physical descent. Very soon, however, he tells them: ὑμεῖς ἐκ τοῦ πατρὸς τοῦ διαβόλου ἐστε (v. 44), obviously switching to spiritual descent; they cannot be Abraham's children because he did not try to kill those who told him the truth. All this suggests that to belong to the Abrahamic family is to believe in Jesus, although the idea of obedience, which epitomises Abraham, is implied. Jesus seems to accept the Jews' claim once more, when he later refers to '*your father* Abraham [who] rejoiced to see my day'. The Pharisees change their position too, for when Jesus suggests that they are not following Abraham but their father (unspecified), they protest: 'We were not born as the result of fornication;[14] we have one Father—even God' (v. 41). Despite the inconsistencies, two types of fatherhood are being juggled here: the Jews may be physical sons of Abraham but true sonship is spiritual and consists in believing, as Abraham did, in Jesus as the *Messiah*. This lengthy passage points up the contrast between spiritual and physical descent enunciated in the Prologue: 'those who believe in his name are born not of blood nor the will of the flesh, but of God' (1:13).

There is a change of subject when Jesus claims that anyone who keeps his word will never see death. In reply, the Jews ask with the same unconscious irony as the woman at the well: 'Are you greater than our father Abraham who died? And the prophets died. Who do you think you are?' (6:53). The Samaritan woman had asked a similar question with regard to Jacob: 'Are you greater than our father Jacob who gave us this well?' (4:12). In asserting an ancestral claim to land, Jesus' interlocutors here are making a racial assertion. They are countered with a breathtaking claim, already discussed: 'Abraham rejoiced to see my day'. They retort that he is not fifty years old yet he claims to have seen Abraham (v. 57). (That is not quite what Jesus had said: it was Abraham who had seen Jesus.) He goes on to make a claim for pre-existence, if not of eternity. It needs to be pointed out that the verbs used in this sentence are different: Αμὴν ἀμὴν λέγω ὑμῖν, πρὶν Ἀβραὰμ γενέσθαι ἐγὼ εἰμί (v. 58). This is not a totally new idea because earlier he has said, 'If you do not believe that *I am* (εἰμί), you will die in your sins' (8:24). It is of course drawing a contrast between the different types of existence enjoyed by Abraham and Jesus which the Pharisees easily grasp. They have already accused Jesus of being a Samaritan, perhaps because he questioned the uniqueness of Jewish prerogatives, as the Samaritans did. Now his claim of pre-existence enrages them even more as they see it as a claim to divinity. It is in effect a restatement of the opening verse of John's Gospel: 'In the beginning was the Word, and the Word was with God and the Word was God'.

---

14   Perhaps a veiled allusion to Jesus' contested paternity.

2. Moses

Moses, unlike Abraham, is not always understood as a person: his name is often shorthand for the Torah. He is invoked mainly as 1) the *Lawgiver*,[15] often to critique the practices of the Jewish rulers, but he is also seen as 2) a *Leader*, which encompasses Liberator (or literally 'bringer-out') and wonder-working Prophet,[16] usually to point up the superiority of the new age, especially in John. His role as Prophet is, I believe, part of the Leader role. The references to 'the prophet' and 'that prophet' in the Gospel and Acts are taken to refer to Deut 18:15: 'Yahweh your God will raise up for you a prophet like me from among you—you shall listen to him'. At the Mount of Transfiguration, a voice from heaven saying 'Listen to him' can be taken as proof that Jesus is the fulfilment of Moses' prophecy. The statement in Deut 18:18 needs to be read alongside that of 34:10–11. Although it does not say that Yahweh will raise up a prophet like Moses, it defines the kind of prophet that Moses was: 'Since then, no prophet has arisen like Moses *on account of all the signs and wonders* which Yahweh sent him to perform'.[17] The promise of a wonder-working prophet is clearly in people's minds in John, as we shall see. John's Gospel downplays Moses in his roles as Lawgiver (in relation to when circumcision could and should be carried out) and as Leader (regarding the gift of manna); the second is even more pronounced, as will be shown.

2.1 Moses as Lawgiver

It is as Lawgiver that Moses is principally seen both in the Old Testament and the New. Moses is often a metonymy for the law that he delivered. Sometimes, however, Yahweh is indicated as the Lawgiver, emphasising Moses' secondary role (e.g., Exod 20:1; 35:1; Ps 78:5).[18] This variation is also seen in the Gospels. As with Abraham, Moses is used both positively and negatively but unlike Abraham, Moses himself—rather than those who claim him—is treated with something short of respect in more than one episode.

2.1.1 Moses as Lawgiver in the Synoptics

The Torah is often termed the law or commandment of Moses; for example: Mary and Joseph carry out the rite of purification 'according to the law of Moses' (Luke 2:22). In some places, the Law is personalised to the person of Moses; for example: 'Moses said: Honour your father and mother' (Mark 7:10). At times, Moses is coupled with the prophets to mean the entire Old Testament: 'Beginning in Moses and all the prophets [Jesus] interpreted in all the scriptures the things concerning himself' (Luke 24:27). No clear distinction is made between the writer of the Law and the Law itself. The most striking personalisation of Moses is found in Mark 10:2–5 and Matt 19:3–8,[19] where the Pharisees ask Jesus, 'Did not Moses command (ἐνετείλατο) to give a certificate of divorce?',[20] and then adds 'Because of the hardness of your hearts, Moses allowed (ἐπέτρεψεν) you to divorce your wives'. The difference between the verbs is significant, the verb used by Jesus suggesting reluctance. Jesus, however, hints at disapproval when he adds: 'But

---

15 Lee, 'Significance', gives Moses three roles: author, actor and lawgiver. I combine *author* and *lawgiver* and make *actor* more specific.
16 Lee uses the term 'healer' but his role is broader than that.
17 Stenschke, 'Jesus as *the* Prophet', 72–73, details the development of the idea of 'the prophet' in early Judaism.
18 In Acts and the Epistles, Moses is sometimes seen as the mediator rather than the giver of the Law. This is most striking in Stephen's concluding remark: 'you who received the law delivered by angels and did not keep it'.
19 Not found in Luke.
20 The Pharisees had initiated the discourse by asking if it was lawful to divorce one's wife. Telford, *Mark*, 139, doubts if the Pharisees would have needed to ask such a question, unless of course it was a trick question.

from the beginning it was not so'. By drawing attention to the ideal and contrasting it with Moses' concession to their hardness of heart, Jesus is making Moses somewhat responsible, although the hearers much more so. It is quite striking that Yahweh is not mentioned; distancing him from the Torah would make it easier to announce its replacement. In Matthew's unique Sermon on the Mount, Jesus is 'the new Moses' issuing modifications to the law given on Sinai, but he uses variations on the expression, 'it has been said' (vv. 21,27,31,33,38,43) rather than mention Moses; this is particularly noticeable in v. 21: Ἠκούσατε ὅτι ἐρρέθη τοῖς ἀρχαίοις. The rationale perhaps is to avoid setting Jesus and Moses directly against each other. In Matthew 23, after conceding that the teachers of the law and the Pharisees sit in Moses' seat, Jesus utters seven woes against them, calling them hypocrites.[21] He thus is able to honour the Law but not those who purport to teach it. In the floating *Pericope Adulterae*, the woman's accusers claim that Moses commanded that such a one should be stoned; Jesus does not disagree but deals with the issue in a very unexpected way (John 8:7).

2.1.2 Moses as Lawgiver in John

Moses in his role as Lawgiver is viewed with much more ambivalence in John than in the Synoptics. There is no hint of Mosaic observance and, strikingly, no Passover hence no Eucharist. Certainly, Jesus goes up to Jerusalem to certain feasts but that is to give him an opportunity to preach to the crowds. Lee argues that Moses is a prototype of the Johannine Jesus; Moses' parallel role points symbolically to Jesus' identity and function. Jesus does not replace Moses; rather the Johannine Moses maintains an ongoing, christological function that endures in the life of the community of faith.[22] But Jesus in some places does replace Moses, as in the Synoptics.

The first reference to Moses contains a motif that occurs in other parts of the Gospel: 'The law was given through (διά) Moses; grace and truth came through (διά) Jesus Christ' (1:17).[23] It is not clear how strong the contrast is meant to be: the same preposition is used and there is no conjunction. There is also a contrast between the two verbs: giving (ἐδόθη) of the Law with the creative bringing into being (ἐγένετο) of grace and truth. Lee does not see a dualism here but a relationship,[24] but relationships are not always ideal. The balance in the verse suggests a polarisation. Painter points out that grace and truth are attributes of God (as in Ps 25:10)[25] and the verse reads as if truth, as well as grace, is the sole prerogative of Jesus. The role of the Law as personified in Moses, is to bear witness to Jesus. This is enunciated in Philip's profession of faith: 'We have found him of whom Moses in the law and the prophets wrote' (1:45) and, after the healing at Bethesda, Jesus tells his detractors: 'If you believed Moses, you would believe me, because he wrote about me' (5:46).[26]

As in the Synoptics, the Jewish rulers are accused of hypocrisy in failing to obey the one they claim to follow; for example, Jesus claims that they seek to kill him and continues: 'Moses gave you the law, yet not one of you keeps the law' (7:19). It is not a denigration of Moses to accuse his followers of hypocrisy but Jesus goes further, in the controversy surrounding the healing at

---

21 In Acts (23:6; 25:5) and in his own writing (Phil 3:5), Paul confesses to have been a 'Pharisee of the Pharisees' and condemns himself and them for persecutionary rigour, not for hypocrisy.
22 Lee, 'Significance', 10.
23 This seems at odds with Matthew's declaration that he had 'not come to abolish the law and the prophets but to fulfil them' (5:17).
24 Lee, 'Significance', 16–17.
25 Painter, 'Matthew and John', 80–81.
26 This is similar to the argument used in relation to Abraham: 'Believe in me because Abraham whom you claim as your father saw my advent, and believed'. The reference to Moses may be an implied reference to 'that prophet'.

Bethesda (5:10–18). Because the rite has to be performed on the eighth day (Lev 12:3, *inter alia*), it sometimes has to take place on the Sabbath. In John's account, Jesus describes circumcision as Mosaic, but retracts this attribution by making it patriarchal, as indeed it is (Gen 17:12). Jesus then goes on to make an invidious comparison: the healing of a body is more commendable than its mutilation, even if commanded: 'Are you angry with me because I healed a man's whole body?' (7:23b). This has the effect of downgrading Moses, as well as countering Jesus' enemies.

2.2. Moses as Leader and Prophet

In the Old Testament, Moses is often depicted as bringing the people of Israel out of Egypt (e.g., in Exodus 3) but in other places Yahweh brings the people out (e.g., Ezekiel 20 *passim*). In all four Gospels, however, Moses is understood as the one who led Israel out of Egypt and performed many miracles.

2.2.1 Moses as Leader in the Synoptics

In all three Synoptics, Jesus uses Moses in a rather rabbinical way in an altercation with the Sadducees concerning the resurrection (Mark 12:26–27, Matt 22:32, Luke 20:37).[27] It is a clear reference to Moses as deliverer, since it is at the burning bush that he received his commission to lead the children of Israel out of Egypt (Exodus 3). Again on the Mount of Transfiguration, Moses is represented as Leader when he appears with Elijah (Mark 9:2–8; Matt 17:1–8; Luke 9:28–36). The two biblical giants are often thought to represent the Old Testament, in its two parts of the Law and the Prophets, but this is untenable.[28] Elijah is not one of the writing prophets;[29] Moses here is not the writer of the Torah but a prophet and a deliverer.

The other appearance of Moses in the role of Leader on the Mount of Transfiguration also echoes the theophany of Mount Sinai; it can be seen as equivalent to entering the Promised Land. In one reading of the narrative in the Pentateuch, the aim was to bring the people of Israel to Sinai, rather than to Canaan.[30] Luke's noting of ἔξοδος as the topic of the conversation among the three (9:31) not only anticipates Jesus' departure but recalls the 'signs and wonders' connected with Moses and Elijah: Moses showed the fathers many miracles (Ps 78:11) and Elijah brought people back to life and called down fire from heaven (I Kgs 17:8–24; 18:36–40). Elijah is the precursor of the Day of the Lord, which embodies both judgment and salvation, as in Malachi's prophecy: 'I will send you Elijah the prophet before the Day of the Lord' (4:5).[31] In Sir 48:10, Elijah is to restore the tribes of Israel, and the *Apocalypse of Elijah* contains the archangel Michael's revelation to Elijah on Mt Carmel. Both Moses and Elijah were also thought to have escaped death (Deut 34:6; 2 Kgs 2:11).[32] Therefore two messianic forerunners appear in conversation with the Messiah. David Moessner links the epiphany with Jesus's final journey to Jerusalem which takes up so much of Luke's Gospel:

---

27 Already discussed in relation to Abraham.
28 Mark puts Elijah first: 'Elijah with Moses' (9:4), perhaps because of the emphasis on Elijah in the next pericope in which the disciples ask Jesus whether Elijah is his forerunner (9:11–13).
29 In fact, in Mark 8:28; Matt 16:14 and Luke 9:19, he is distinct from 'one of the prophets'.
30 Craghan, 'Exodus', 424. Elijah too had an epiphany on Mt Horeb (1 Kings 19) though it was on Mt Carmel that he prevailed over the priests of Baal.
31 It is in this context that Malachi refers to Elijah and why John is seen as Elijah in the Synoptics. Elijah and John sought to turn the hearts of the people of Israel to the Lord from Baalism and Pharisaism, respectively.
32 In Gabriel's message to Elizabeth (Luke 1:17), Elijah is both himself and John the Baptiser. Yet John denies that he is Elijah in John 1:21; this is literally true, of course!

This great journey from the mount of revelation to Israel's 'central place' brings Israel's first exodus to its intended goal when Jesus will die, like Moses, and be taken up, like Elijah, in bringing the longed-for life of release and redemption and worship in the land of promise to its completion.[33]

2.2.2 Moses as Leader in John

On two occasions, John uses Moses's actions in the desert of Sinai to highlight Jesus' mission. The first is positive: 'As Moses lifted up the serpent in the wilderness, just so must the son of man be lifted up' (John 3:14). The gift of eternal life is compared with the prolongation of earthly life which the sight of the bronze serpent conveyed. The serpent is called 'the symbol of salvation' in *The Wisdom of Solomon*,[34] and the rather tenuous connection between Moses and Christ is to be found in the granting of salvation through a 'raising up'. The comparison, however, seems lopsided: the conjunction καθώς equates the crucifixion with an act of sympathetic magic which later developed into a form of idolatry and led Hezekiah to break 'Nehushtan' in pieces (2 Kgs 18:4).[35]

The second comparison is more polemical. After the feeding of the five thousand, the people initially exclaim, 'This is indeed the prophet that is to come into the world' (6:14).[36]

But by the next day their attitude has changed. Absurdly, they ask for a sign to rival the gift of manna to their fathers in the wilderness; the prediction, in Bar 29:8, that manna will recur in the Messianic age may lie behind this challenge. Jesus seems to take the quotation, '*He* gave them bread from heaven to eat', as if *he* is Moses, not Yahweh, because he retorts: 'It was not Moses who gave you the bread from heaven', though they had not made such a claim. The remark that follows, 'My Father gives you the *true* bread from heaven', has the effect of downgrading the manna even further. This exchange is a clear echo of the contrast of 1:17.

The people make another identification of 'the prophet' on the last day of the Feast of Tabernacles: some react to Jesus' promise of living water with the exclamation: 'This is really the prophet' (7:40).[37] It is very significant that the crowd, acting—as they often do—somewhat as a Greek chorus, twice mentions 'the prophet' after two incidents which parallel two of Moses' great feats in the desert: providing manna from heaven and living water from the rock. Thus the only two clear claims that Jesus is 'the prophet' are from the crowd, not from Jesus himself or the evangelist.[38] It is true that, early in the Gospel, the priests and Levites ask John the Baptiser if he is Elijah or the Prophet and he answers in the negative (1:22) but he does not point them elsewhere. In Acts, however, Peter mentions Moses' prophecy in his address after the healing of the lame man: 'Moses said, The Lord God will raise up a prophet from your brethren as he raised me up' (3:22). He is seeking to prove Jesus' messiahship by ranging across the Old Testament from Abraham to Samuel.

---

33 Moessner, *Luke the Historian*, 319.
34 'When the horrible fierceness of the creatures came upon them, and they perished with the stings of crooked serpents, your anger did not last forever; but they were troubled for a season that they might be admonished, having a sign of salvation, to put them in remembrance of your law' (Wis 16:5–6).
35 The rabbis maintained that the serpent itself did not cure; as long as Israel looked upward and submitted their minds to their Father in Heaven, they were cured (Solomon, *Talmud*, 244).
36 Lierman, 'The New Testament Moses', 318, argues that John 6 (and Mark 6:34–44) are saturated with allusions to Jesus' kingship. But after the people are miraculously fed, the people do not say, 'This is indeed *the king* who is to come into the world' but *'the prophet'* (John 6:14).
37 Others claim that he is the Messiah and the conversation turns to David and Bethlehem.
38 Stenschke, 'Jesus as *the* Prophet', 74n, believes that the evangelists' reluctance to identify Jesus with 'the prophet' may be the use of the trope by contemporary charismatic figures, as recorded by Josephus.

3. Abraham and Moses

Abraham and Moses are mentioned together on several occasions, with approbation. In the second half of the Dives and Lazarus allegory, Abraham directs the rich man to Moses and the prophets. Abraham is used as a mouthpiece for Jesus' own teaching about the fixity of the last state and particularly the sufficiency of the Old Testament: nothing is necessary apart from Scripture, yet that will not be sufficient for those who refuse to believe. Abraham encourages Dives' brothers to read Moses and the prophets, presumably because they denounce the rich and exalt the poor. The anachronism of Abraham's appeal to Moses and the writing prophets who came many centuries after him indicates that it is not the historical figure that speaks but an omniscient personage from outside time.

In a pericope found in all three Synoptics, Jesus mentions both Abraham and Moses in a dispute in which Sadducees pose the conundrum concerning seven brothers who marry the same woman: 'In the resurrection, whose husband will she be?' (Mark 12:18–27;[39] Matt 22:23–33; Luke 20:27–38). Jesus does not answer the question but accuses the Sadducees of not knowing what the Scriptures teach about the resurrection; therefore their question is based on a false premise. He refers to the encounter in the desert where Yahweh defines himself as 'the God of Abraham, Isaac and Jacob' (Exod 3:6). Although, in all three accounts, the Sadducees mention Moses in their question, Matthew has Jesus reply, 'Have you not read what was said by *God*?' (v. 31b); this is very different from Matthew's failure, in the Sermon on the Mount, to attribute the Law even to Moses. Despite variations in the Synoptic accounts, all agree on Jesus' argument that the fathers had been long dead when God spoke to Moses but he could not be their God if they no longer existed; therefore they must live in an unspecified sense. This is a decidedly rabbinical argument, turning on the use of the present tense.[40] In the background is the declaration that the exodus is the fulfilment of a promise made to the patriarchs, a point made often in Acts but nowhere else in the Gospels, which is somewhat surprising. Jesus' use of Abraham, Isaac and Jacob to argue for the afterlife and the immortality of the soul has similarities with Jesus' use of the refrain, ἐγώ εἰμί in John 8, to assert his pre-existence and, obliquely, his divinity.

There is another connection between Abraham and Moses which is not immediately obvious. On two separate occasions in John's Gospel, Jesus condemns his enemies for seeking to kill him; he does this by enlisting Moses against his false disciples and Abraham against his false sons. First, the Pharisees' murderous intent is because he healed a man on the Sabbath (7:19,22); in the second incident, their sin is their failure to believe in him (8:37–47). It is easy to see that killing is contrary to Moses' commandment but the line, 'Abraham did not do such things' (8:40b), is more obscure. It seems that the motivation behind their murderous rage explains the contrast with Abraham: the Pharisees seek to kill Jesus because they are unwilling to hear the truth that he brings from God, but Abraham was not guilty of such a failure: 'he saw my day and rejoiced' (8:57). Jesus points out the hypocrisy of those who claim to be Moses' disciples and those who claim to be Abraham's descendants and yet seek an opportunity to kill him.

Abraham and Moses, nevertheless, are implicitly contrasted in Matthew and John, with different speakers and in different contexts. In denying that these two evangelists are anti-Judaic, Christopher J. Probst argues that the Jesus that they present is an internal critic, and therefore resembles one of the *nevi'im* of old[41] (the description also aptly fits John the Baptiser). John's

---

39 This is the only reference to Abraham in the whole of Mark.
40 This is not in the Hebrew, but is in the Septuagint.
41 Probst, 'Anti-Judaism', 1.

Jesus certainly uses the language of the prophets in denying the Pharisees' claim to be Abraham's descendants and calling them at one point children of the devil (8:44). Matthew's Jesus also calls them γεννήματα ἐχιδνῶν (12:34; 23:33) as does the Baptiser (Matt 3:7). Whether the critique of the Pharisees in the Gospels is totally justified is a separate issue, but there can be little doubt that the criticism is transferred to Moses himself in John, if not in Matthew. Few 'nevi'im of old' criticised the Mosaic law in the way that Jesus and John the Baptiser do, exceptions being perhaps Jer 7:22–23 and Isa 1:11,14.

We must go to the Pauline Epistles to find instances where Abraham (symbolising faith) and Moses (embodying the law) are explicitly set over against each other. In his sermon at the synagogue in Pisidian Antioch, Paul addresses the listeners, including the God-fearers present, as brothers in Abraham: Ἄνδρες ἀδελφοί, υἱοὶ γένους Ἀβραὰμ καὶ οἱ ἐν ὑμῖν φοβούμενοι τὸν θεόν (Acts 13:26). The same rationale may be behind the contrast between the Abrahamic faith and Mosaic law in the epistles. In Romans, Paul asserts that 'Moses wrote that the one who practises the righteousness which is based on the law will live by it' (10:5), whereas in his treatment of Abraham, he has already concluded that 'the just shall live by faith' (1:17). This echoes John 1:17, where Jesus and grace take the place of Abraham and faith. In Galatians the theological argument is very similar to that made by John at the Jordan and Jesus throughout John 8: οἱ ἐκ πίστεως, οὗτοι υἱοί εἰσιν Ἀβραάμ (3:7). Paul then goes on to juxtapose Abraham and Moses: 'The law which came 430 years afterward does not annul a covenant previously certified by God' (3:17).

4. Conclusion

There are similarities and differences in the way that both Abraham and Moses are regarded and used in the Gospels. Abraham without exception is regarded positively in both his roles as covenant partner and universal Father, but he is used negatively in his role as Father. Moses on the other hand, is considered positively and negatively in both his roles as Lawgiver and Leader, mainly against the Pharisees.

Abraham's role as *covenant partner* is lauded in the Canticles by Mary and Zechariah. His *fatherhood* extends to Gentiles at the messianic banquet which is found in all three Synoptics, and to outcasts and Gentiles in Luke. But his role as Father in John the Baptiser's address in Matthew and Luke is used against the religious rulers of Israel or the crowds by pointing out that they are false sons. In Matthew, John the Baptiser uses lack of repentance and, in John, Jesus invokes unbelief to attack the Pharisees. In Luke, Abraham, as Father and Warden of Paradise, denies Dives entry to paradise because of his lack of compassion. This contrasts with Zacchaeus who is able to make restitution.

Across the four Gospels, there appears to be an intensification in the negativity in which Abraham is used. Mark is largely lacking in controversy: Abraham, along with Isaac and Jacob, is mentioned only once, in the message to Moses at the burning bush, in common with Matthew and Luke. Luke records a measure of conflict in John the Baptiser's diatribe where he uses Abraham against the crowds. The controversy becomes more intense in Matthew, because John the Baptiser's diatribe is against the Pharisees and Sadducees, rather than the crowds. But it is in John's Gospel that the dispute with the synagogue reaches its peak in the extended dialogue where Jesus not only denies that the Pharisees are sons of Abraham but calls them children of the devil.

Moses' roles as *Lawgiver* and *Leader* are similarly used positively and negatively. He is regarded positively as the Lawgiver on many occasions: when Mary and Joseph go to the Temple for the rite of purification; when Jesus tells lepers to report to the priest, and when he tells the people that their leaders sit in Moses' seat and they should do as they say (but not do as they do). The most laudatory use of Moses is in the allegory of Dives and Lazarus where Abraham gives his imprimatur twice to the Torah and the Nevi'im: 'They have Moses and the prophets: let them hear them' (16:29,31). He is regarded positively as Leader when his raising of the bronze serpent is used as a type of the crucifixion. He is used as a weapon many times to entrap or mock the Pharisees as hypocrites and false disciples. But the role of Moses himself as the Lawgiver is downplayed by omission in the Sermon on the Mount, and explicitly in John when circumcision is compared unfavourably with a miracle of healing. His role as Leader is devalued when the manna which did not save from death is contrasted with the bread from heaven. It is somewhat surprising that Moses' role as Deliverer is neglected in the Gospels in favour of Lawgiver.

As with Abraham, there seems to be an intensification of negativity with regard to Moses from Mark to Luke to Matthew to John. Mark mentions Moses twice, neutrally in the pericope about the bush and less favourably in the interchange with the Pharisees about divorce, where all the Synoptics contrast Moses' concession to their hardness of heart with the situation that prevailed in the Garden of Eden. Luke's only reference to Moses as Leader is at the Transfiguration where his position is clearly one of great honour, as is his role as Lawgiver in the allegory of Dives and Lazarus. But Matthew's Sermon on the Mount contains an implicit downgrading of the Mosaic Law in comparison with Jesus' teaching. It is overt in John, however, with regard to the institution of circumcision and especially the gift of manna.

The perception of Moses, therefore, differs from that of Abraham; Moses himself is sometimes an ambivalent figure. There is a possible explanation for this: whereas the Abrahamic covenant is easily incorporated into Christian salvation history, there is a perceived discontinuity between the Mosaic covenant and the new covenant which Jesus ushers in. There is tension because the Christian communities are still working out just what the relationship is with Judaism, as shown in the Council in Jerusalem recorded in Acts 15. Abraham's fatherhood is universal and can only be alienated by lack of that faith which is open even to the Gentiles. But Moses cannot be the universal Lawgiver or even universal Leader, because of the ethnic connection. Abraham's fatherhood could more easily be made relevant to the Gentiles, hence Paul's insistence that Abraham is 'the father of us all' (Rom 4:16). Despite the negativity, both Abraham and Moses play a role in authenticating Jesus' claims: Abraham was an ancestor who rejoiced to see Jesus' day; Moses promised a wonder-working prophet that God would raise up for his people. But Abraham is more easily incorporated into salvation history; as Gentiles flooded into the Church, he eclipsed Moses almost totally.

Bibliography

Barth, K.	*Church Dogmatics* 4.3.1 (Edinburgh: T&T Clark, 1961).
Bauckham, R.	'Jesus and the Eyewitnesses, Fourteen Years Later', *JGAR* 3 (2019), 5–14.
Bauckham, R.	'The Rich Man and Lazarus: The Parable and the Parallels', *NTS* 37.2 (1999), 225–46.
Craghan, J.	'Exodus', in *International Bible Commentary* (Collegeville, MN: The Liturgical Press, 1998), 396–445.
Green, J.	*Conversion in Luke–Acts: Divine Action, Human Cognition and the People of God* (Grand Rapids, MI: Baker Academic, 2015).
Hagner, D.	*How New Is the New Testament?: First-Century Judaism and the Emergence of Christianity* (Ada, MI: Baker Academic, 2018).
Lee, D.	'The Significance of Moses in the Gospel of John', *Australian Biblical Review* 63 (2015), 52–66. (online, 1–17). https://repository.divinity.edu.au/2880/1/D.Lee%252C_Moses%252C_ABR.pdf [accessed 13 July, 2020]
Lierman, J.	'The New Testament Moses in the Context of Ancient Judaism', *Tyndale Bulletin* 53.2 (2002), 317–20.
Moessner, D.	*Luke the Historian of Israel's Legacy, Theologian of Israel's 'Christ'* (Berlin: De Gruyter, 2016).
Painter, J.	'Matthew and John', in David C. Sim & Boris Repschinski (eds.), *Matthew and his Christian Contemporaries* (London: T&T Clark, 2008), 66–86.
Parsons, M.	'"Short in Stature": Luke's Physical Description of Zacchaeus', *NTS* 47.1 (2001), 50–57.
Probst, C.	'Anti-Judaism and the Gospel of John', *Reformed Perspectives Magazine*, 4.2 (2002), 1–26. https://thirdmill.org/magazine/article.asp/link/chr_probst%5ENT.Probst.anti_judaism.john.html/at/Anti-Judaism%20and%20the%20Gospel%20of%20John [Accessed 13 July 2020]
Solomon, N. (ed.).	*The Talmud: A Selection* (London: Penguin, 2009).
Stenschke, C.	'Jesus as *the* Prophet according to Deuteronomy 18:15–22', *JGAR* 3 (2019), 69–86.
Telford, W.	*Mark* (Sheffield: Sheffield Academic Press, 1995).
Vawter, B.	'The Gospel according to John', *Jerome Biblical Commentary, Vol. 2*. (London: Geoffrey Chapman, 1984), 414–466.
Vermes, G.	*The Complete Dead Sea Scrolls in English* (London: Penguin, 1997).

Re-naming the Toll Collector in Matthew 9:9
A review of the options

MICHAEL J. KOK

Abstract

In contrast to the Synoptic parallels (cf. Mark 2:14; Luke 5:27), Matthew 9:9 specifies that it was Matthew, instead of Levi the son of Alphaeus, who was sitting at a 'toll booth' (τελώνιον) in Capernaum. Matthew 10:3 reinforces this point by attaching the label 'the toll collector' (ὁ τελώνης) to Matthew's name. This article will review the various scholarly explanations for these two redactional changes. It will defend the position that the anonymous Gospel writer transferred Levi's call narrative over to Matthew because it was believed that they both had worked in the same general occupation. Further, the evangelist deemed it necessary to narrate how Matthew completely abandoned this notorious profession, even though the exact details of how Matthew became a disciple of Jesus had long been forgotten, since his former means of livelihood is strongly condemned in passages that are unique to the first canonical Gospel.

Key Words: Matthew, Levi, Papias, authorship, toll collector

Exegetes continue to debate the reason(s) for why the author of the first canonical Gospel[1] changed the name of Levi to Matthew (Matt. 9:9; contra Mark 2:14; Luke 5:27) and appended 'the toll collector' (ὁ τελώνης) to Matthew's name (Matt. 10:3; contra Mark 3:18; Luke 6:15; Acts 1:13).[2] Commentators have offered the following suggestions to explicate the evangelist's redactional activity in these verses:[3]

1. the toll collector Levi was rightly identified by his alternate name Matthew;
2. the apostle Matthew had connections with the postulated Matthean community or was the source of certain traditions incorporated into the Gospel of Matthew;

---

[1] Although the authorship of this canonical text is technically anonymous, I will designate it by its traditional title, namely the 'Gospel according to Matthew' (εὐαγγέλιον κατὰ Μαθθαῖον), as a matter of convenience.

[2] Τελώνης should be translated as 'toll collector' and denoted someone who collected duties at major travel points such as Capernaum, where goods were transported between the territories of Philip and Antipas. See Donahue, 'Tax Collectors and Sinners', 42–49, 59; cf. Keener, *The Gospel of Matthew*, 292–93.

[3] For a convenient summary of the interpretive options, see Gnilka, *Das Matthäusevangelium*, 1.330–31; Davies and Allison, *Matthew VIII–XVII*, 98–99. Below, I also engage Benjamin Bacon's case that the changes in these two verses were based on nothing more than a scribal error. See Bacon, *Studies in Matthew*, 39–40.

3. the so-called Gospel of Matthew was pseudonymously ascribed to the evangelist Matthew and the verses in 9:9 and 10:3 contributed to the authorial fiction;
4. the Matthean Jesus only had a circle of 'twelve disciples' (cf. Matt. 10:1; 11:1; 20:17) and this necessitated the replacement of Levi with one of the Twelve; or
5. the call narrative of Levi was transferred over to Matthew because the latter had a similar occupation as the former.

There are strengths and weaknesses to each of these scholarly proposals. Be that as it may, the strong likelihood that Matthew 9:9 copied the story in Mark 2:14 about Jesus's command to Levi, originally a separate character from Matthew, to abandon his 'toll booth' (τελώνιον) weighs against the notions that Matthew was either the evangelist or one of the evangelist's informants. The most plausible solution may be that there was a hazy memory that Matthew was previously employed as a toll collector, but the evangelist borrowed the details from the Markan pericope to fill in the gaps that were forgotten over time about how Matthew was elected for the office of an 'apostle' (ἀπόστολος). Furthermore, by comparing the Matthean *Sondergut*, or special material, to the Synoptic triple and double tradition material, it seems clear that impenitent 'toll collectors' (τελῶναι) are depicted fairly negatively in the Gospel of Matthew. For this reason, the evangelist stressed that Matthew left his former profession behind to become a follower of Jesus.

An Authorial Tradition?

Commentators who uphold the ecclesiastical tradition about Matthean authorship and read Matthew 9:9 as a description of the evangelist's own conversion generally assume that the evangelist had to be fluent in Greek due to the demands of his job.[4] For Leon Morris, this is complemented by the evangelist's significant interest in gold, silver and currency ranging from the *assarion*, the *chalkos*, the *denarius*, the *didrachma*, the *kodrantes*, and the *stater*.[5] The latter observation, though, does not require that the evangelist was a toll collector and may not be any more convincing than the efforts to show that the third canonical Gospel was written by Luke the physician (cf. Col. 4:14) due to the alleged utilization of medical vocabulary in the text.[6] Finally, with regards to the question about why an eyewitness to the ministry of Jesus relied on the reports about it from a non-eyewitness like Mark, given the supposition of Markan priority,[7] these commentators often answer that Matthew was actually relying on Peter's apostolic witness that was mediated through Mark's Gospel.[8] Again, this answer may only be persuasive to scholars who are already persuaded by Papias of Hierapolis on the origins of Mark's Gospel as a record of Peter's

---

4 For example, see Gundry, *The Use of the Old Testament*, 183; Hill, *The Gospel of Matthew*, 1; Mounce, *Matthew*, 1; France, *Matthew*, 67–68; Morris, *The Gospel according to Matthew*, 14; Blomberg, *Matthew*, 43; Hagner, *Matthew 1–13*, lxxvi; Carson, *Matthew*, 18–19; Osborne, *Matthew*, 34; Powers, *The Progressive Publication of Matthew*, 28–29.
5 Morris, *Matthew*, 14 n.46.
6 See the refutation of Hobart, *The Medical Language*, in Cadbury, *The Style and Literary Method*, 39–72.
7 I affirm the scholarly consensus on Markan priority based on the cumulative arguments from length, order, grammar, style, and content. Note, however, the objection of Powers (*The Progressive Publication of Matthew*, 49), a proponent of Matthean priority, that 'a view about Gospel sequence is not a valid reason for rejecting apostolic authorship'.
8 For example, see Mounce, *Matthew*, 2; France, *Matthew*, 73–74; Blomberg, *Matthew*, 43–44; Gundry, *Matthew*, 621–22; Carson, *Matthew*, 18; Osborne, *Matthew*, 34; Brown and Roberts, *Matthew*, 16.

preaching (cf. Eusebius, *H.E.* 3.39.15; cf. Acts 12:5; 1 Pet 5:13).[9]

If Matthew 9:9 is taken at face value, there needs to be some hypothesis for why Mark 2:14 and Luke 5:27 referred to the toll collector stationed in Capernaum as Levi. The traditional view, though it was not held unanimously (e.g., Clement, *Str.* 4.9; Origen, *Cels.* 1.62), was that the same person bore the Semitic names Levi and Matthew. An idea that was frequently touted in the Patristic period was that the evangelists Mark and Luke wrote down Matthew's less-well-known name Levi because they did not want to bring the Apostle into disrepute, but Matthew was humble enough to own up to his past misdeeds under the name by which he was popularly known to his readers (e.g., John Chrysostom, *Hom. in Mt.* 30.1; Jerome, *Matt.* 1.9.9).[10] Now, it is true that there were examples of individuals with a Jewish name and Greek or Latin cognomen such as John/Mark (Acts 12:12), Saul/Paul (Acts 13:9), or Jesus/Justus (Col. 4:11).[11] The second option is that Jesus conferred a new nickname on Levi, since Mattaniah or Mattithiah means 'gift of Yahweh', and this may parallel how Simon and Joseph were given epithets such as 'rock' (cf. Matt. 16:18; John 1:42) and 'son of encouragement' respectively (cf. Acts 4:36).[12] W. F. Albright and C. S. Mann recommend a third option, which is that the toll-collector Matthew had Levitical tribal origins, but a translator of an Aramaic source confused the term 'Levite' with the personal name 'Levi' due to the absence of an article before לוי.[13]

Each of these hypotheses runs into difficulties. First, Richard Bauckham points out that it was 'virtually unparalleled' for a first-century Palestinian Jew to bear two common Semitic names, for, in Tal Ilan's lexicon of Jewish names from 330 BCE to 200 CE, Matthew was the ninth most popular name and Levi the seventeenth most popular.[14] In the search for parallels for this rare phenomenon, William L. Lane documents three examples from Nabatean inscriptions.[15] Bauckham dismisses Lane's evidence as irrelevant for Jewish practice[16] and, after uncovering five potential Jewish parallels, he proceeds to demonstrate why each one is not applicable to the case for the same Jewish person being named Levi and Matthew.[17] Second, the evangelist's tendency was to write ὁ λεγόμενος ('the one who is called') when dealing with surnames and epithets (cf Matt. 1:16; 4:18; 10:2; 26:3,14), which can be observed in references such as Jesus who is called 'Christ' (Χριστός; cf. 1:16) or Simon who is called 'Peter' (Πέτρος; cf. 4:18; 10:2), but the article

---

9   For a review of scholarship, see Kok, *The Gospel on the Margins*, 19–105. For a recent defence of Mark's Petrine authorship not covered in this monograph, see Bond, 'Was Peter behind Mark's Gospel', 46–61.
10 See Simonetti, *Matthew 1–13*, 177; Luz, *Matthew 1–8*, 32 n.12; Boxall, *Matthew through the Centuries*, 31, 172.
11 For scholars who emphasise the relevance of these parallels, see Mounce, *Matthew*, 83; France, *Matthew*, 69, 69 n.54; Morris, *Matthew*, 219; Blomberg, *Matthew*, 155; Gundry, *Matthew*, 166; Hagner, *Matthew 1–13*, 238; Carson, *Matthew*, 224; Witherington, *Matthew*, 197; Osborne, Matthew, 334.
12 For example, see Mounce, *Matthew*, 83; Blomberg, *Matthew*, 155; Gundry, *Matthew*, 166; Hagner, *Matthew 1–13*, 238; Witherington, *Matthew*, 197; Osborne, *Matthew*, 334.
13 Albright & Mann, *Matthew*, clxxvii; cf. Gundry, *The Use of the Old Testament*, 183; idem, *Matthew*, 166; Witherington, *Matthew*, 197; Powers, *The Progressive Publication of Matthew*, 51.
14 Bauckham, *Eyewitnesses*, 109–10; cf. Ilan, *Lexicon of Jewish Names*.
15 Lane, *The Gospel of Mark*, 100–101 n.29. Honainu, the son of Aba, who is surnamed Abdallahi, Martai who is surnamed Zabdath, and Malku who is surnamed Bashamah are listed as the three examples.
16 Bauckham, *Eyewitnesses*, 109 n.54.
17 Bauckham, *Eyewitnesses*, 109–10. The five examples are Simon who had the additional name Benaiah or the epithet 'the builder', Joseph who had the additional name Zaboud, Judah who had the additional name Addan or Annan, Petahiah who had the additional name Mordecai, and Tehina who had the additional name Eleazar. Yet Bauckham objects that the first and fourth examples may involve nicknames, the second example may be a Nabatean name that a Jew living in Nabatea might have adopted, and the third and fifth examples derive from late and unreliable sources (cf. Epiphanius, *Haer.* 15.2.1; *Sifre Deut.* 240).

is not used in 9:9.[18] Third, the flaw in Albright and Mann's theory is that none of the Synoptics explicitly dubs Matthew as a Levite (i.e. Matt. 9:9; 10:3; Mark 3:18; Luke 6:15; cf. Acts 1:13), so their conjectured Aramaic source must have left the Levite unnamed (cf. Mark 2:14; Luke 5:27).[19] They also reckon that there were more Levites than were needed to perform services at the Jerusalem Temple, forcing Matthew to seek out alternative means of employment that alienated him from the religious establishment,[20] but this historical reconstruction is speculative.[21]

It is difficult to escape the conclusion that two different individuals, namely Matthew and Levi the son of Alphaeus, were conflated in Matthew 9:9. This renders the identification of the evangelist as Matthew unlikely, for Matthew could have retold his own experience of how he met Jesus instead of copying Mark 2:14. This leads to the next option that Levi was exchanged for Matthew due to the evangelist's high regard for Matthew as either the founder of the Christ congregations to whom this Gospel was addressed or as the composer of one of the Gospel's main sources.[22] If Papias's contention about Matthew's λόγια or 'oracles' (in Eusebius, *H.E.* 3.39.16) was later misread in reference to our first canonical Gospel (e.g., Irenaeus, *Haer.* 3.1.1; Eusebius, *H.E.* 3.24.6; 6.25.4), Papias may have been alluding to a testimonium source or collection of messianic prophecies,[23] to the hypothetical sources underlying the Synoptic double tradition or the special Matthean material,[24] or to a lost Jewish Gospel. James R. Edwards has revived the ancient hypothesis that Matthew was the author of the *Gospel according to the Hebrews* (cf. Epiphanius, *Haer.* 29.9.4; 30.3.7; 30.13.2; 30.14.3; Jerome, *Epist.* 20.5; *Vir. ill.* 3; *Tract. Ps.* 135; *Matt.* 12.13; *Is.* 11.1–3; *Pelag.* 3.2), a text which Eusebius (*H.E.* 3.39.17) claimed that Papias was familiar with, and conjectures that our extant Greek Gospel of Matthew was named after the apostle who had such a formative influence on the Jewish-Christian tradition.[25]

It is beyond the purposes of this essay to determine the precise referent behind Papias's notice about Matthew's 'oracles'. Nonetheless, the brief mention of Matthew in 9:9 seems like an obscure way of signalling one's debt to a key source. This could be contrasted to the explicit declaration in the Johannine epilogue that the beloved disciple was 'the one who wrote these things' (ὁ γράψας ταῦτα). John 21:24 promotes an authorship claim: it does not merely recognize that the beloved disciple's teachings influenced the shape of the Johannine tradition, but credits this figure with writing the central contents of the fourth canonical Gospel.[26] On the contrary, there is no indication in

---

18   Pesch, 'Levi-Matthäus', 47; Luz, *Matthew 8–20*, 32 n.13, n.21.
19   France, *Matthew*, 70.
20   Albright & Mann, *Matthew*, clxxviii–clxxxiv.
21   France, *Matthew*, 70.
22   For instance, see Pesch, 'Levi-Matthäus', 56; Gundry, *The Use of the Old Testament*, 184; Hill, *Matthew*, 53–54, 173; Gnilka, *Das Matthäusevangelium*, 1.331; Davies and Allison, *Matthew VIII–XVII*, 99; Hagner, *Matthew 1-13*, xlvi; Blomberg, *Matthew*, 44; Carter, *Matthew*, 23; Nolland, *Matthew*, 3–4; Witherington, *Matthew*, 5, 29; Keener, *Matthew*, 40; Bauckham, *Eyewitnesses*, 111.
23   Rendel, 'The "Logia"', 341–348; Grant, *The Gospels*, 65, 144.
24   Schleiermacher, 'Über die Zeugnisse des Papias', 735–68; Manson, *Studies in the Gospels*, 77–87; Hill, *Matthew*, 24-27; Davies & Allison, *Matthew I–VII*, 17; Black, 'The Use of Rhetorical Terminology', 32–35; Hagner, *Matthew 1-13*, xlv-xlvi; Nolland, *Matthew*, 3; MacDonald, *Two Shipwrecked Gospels*, 15.
25   Edwards, *The Hebrew Gospel*, 2–10, 256. For scholars who believe that Papias's assumption that Matthew's Gospel was a translation was based on confusing it with another Semitic Gospel, see France, *Evangelist and Teacher*, 64–66; Hagner, *Matthew 1-13*, xlv; Bauckham, *Eyewitnesses*, 224. For criticism of dating the Jewish Christian Gospels that were referenced by Patristic writers under the title of the *Gospel according to the Hebrews* to the time of Papias, see Kok, 'Did Papias of Hierapolis Use', 29–53.
26   Bauckham, *Eyewitnesses*, 359–63, rebuts the frequent appeal to John 19:19, where it is stated that Pilate 'wrote' (ἔγραψεν) the inscription posted on the cross when he really had his subordinates inscribe the words on the titulus, for John 19:19 means that the precise words were inscribed at Pilate's dictation.

Matthew 9:9 or 10:3 that Matthew penned any of the Jesus traditions. This counts against George D. Kilpatrick's thesis that these two verses were inserted into the text to supplement the pseudonymous ascription of this Gospel to Matthew as well.[27] In Bart Ehrman's taxonomy of pseudonymity in the ancient world, there is a distinction between deliberate forgery and false attributions to anonymous literary works.[28] The Gospel 'according to Matthew' (κατὰ Μαθθαῖον) may be an example of the latter and Matthew was probably neither the author of it nor of its written sources.

The authorial tradition attached to the first canonical Gospel may have initially arisen out of an early attempt to resolve the contradiction between Matthew 9:9 and Mark 2:14, possibly at a date before Luke's Gospel was either published or circulated, as Luke 5:27 would have offered additional support for Mark 2:14. Some Christian readers may have surmised that Matthew was the author of the first canonical Gospel because he supposedly correctly identified himself in Matthew 9:9, which also means that they may have deduced that Mark simply made a mistake in erroneously calling the toll collector Levi. After all, second-century Christian writers did not hesitate to denigrate Mark's work when it was compared to the high standards set by Matthew, such as Papias's informant who contrasted the lack of 'order' (τάξις) in Mark's Gospel with Matthew's carefully arranged composition (cf. Eusebius, *H.E.* 3.39.15–16).[29] It may have only been at a later time, when the Gospels of Mark and Matthew were placed on the same level of canonical authority, that efforts were made to harmonize Mark 2:14 and Matthew 9:9 rather than just view the latter as more accurate than the former.

An Alternative Solution?

I will now turn to the alternative theories that aim to account for why Matthew was substituted for Levi in Matthew 9:9. The call of Levi to discipleship in Mark 2:14 closely resembles Jesus's summons to the first four apostles in Mark 1:16–20. Indeed, a scribe who was unaware of the conflation of Levi with Matthew in Matthew 9:9 introduced the Latinized λεββαῖος into the list of the Twelve in the textual variant in Mark 3:18 (D).[30] Rudolf Pesch goes further by arguing that Jesus's 'disciples' (μαθηταί) were exclusively equated with the circle of the Twelve in Matthew's Gospel.[31] Hence, Levi, now renamed Matthew, had to be one of the twelve apostles. Pesch made three additional observations about how the author of Matthew's Gospel edited the names in the Markan source. First, he or she deleted names that the readers may have been unfamiliar with such as Jairus (9:18; cf. Mark 5:22), Bartimaeus (9:27; cf. Mark 10:46), and Alexander and Rufus (27:32; cf. Mark 15:21).[32] Second, he or she made corrections such as modifying the spelling of Ἰωσῆς (Mark 6:3; 15:40) to Ἰωσήφ (Matt. 13:55; 27:56).[33] Third, in a similar case to Matthew 9:9, he or she swapped Salome in Mark 16:1 with the unnamed mother of the sons of Zebedee in Matthew 27:56 (cf. Matt. 20:21).[34]

The premise of Pesch's argument that whenever a 'disciple' (μαθητής) is mentioned in Matthew's Gospel, one of the twelve apostles is implied, may be questionable (cf. Matt. 8:21).[35] If

---

27 Kilpatrick, *The Origins of the Gospel*, 138–39.
28 Ehrman, *Forgery and Counterforgery*, 43–67.
29 See Kok, *Margins*, 185–227.
30 For this explanation of this textual variant, see Lindars, 'Matthew, Levi, Lebbaeus', 220–22.
31 Pesch, 'Levi-Matthäus', 50–53.
32 Pesch, 'Levi-Matthäus', 53.
33 Pesch, 'Levi-Matthäus', 53–54.
34 Pesch, 'Levi-Matthäus', 54–55. Gundry, *Matthew*, 166, denies that Matthew 27:56 offers a true parallel to the redactional change in Matthew 9:9 because the mother of the sons of Zebedee remains unnamed.
35 Gundry, *Matthew*, 166; Carson, *Matthew*, 223–24; Luz, *Matthew 8–20*, 32 n.16.

the evangelist accepted that there was an extended circle of disciples or followers of Jesus outside of the Twelve, then there was no necessity to switch Levi with one of the twelve apostles. Second, as for the question about why Matthew in particular was chosen to replace Levi, Pesch allows that Matthew may have been a special authority for the Matthean community.[36] On the other hand, Francis Wright Beare and John P. Meier suspect that Matthew was randomly selected from the list of apostolic names in Matthew 10:2–4 because he was as good a candidate as any of the rest of them.[37] Meier adds that there is no proof that Matthew had lived in the area where the author or the original recipients of the Gospel were located, which is often thought to be Antioch in the province of Syria.[38] Moreover, if the author or the intended audience of the Gospel were on personal terms with Matthew, the apostle could have related his own memories to them about the moment when he first met Jesus.[39]

Consequently, Pesch's theory still fails to account for why Matthew was singled out from the group of the apostles.[40] To solve this problem, Mark Kiley notes the assonance between the name 'Matthew' (Μαθθαῖος) and the term for 'disciple' (μαθητής). In the larger pericope in Matthew 9:9–13, Jesus's exhortation 'now go learn' (πορευθέντες δὲ μάθετε) in 9:13 is not found in the Synoptic parallels. Kiley noticed that the verb ἀναγινώσκω (read) could have been employed when Jesus urged the Pharisees to check out Hosea 6:6 (e.g., 12:3, 5, 7), but μανθάνω ('learn') emphasized the process of training to become a disciple, so Matthew represented the ideal of a 'learning disciple'.[41] However, the flaw in Kiley's solution is that neither the narrator nor the Matthean Jesus ever expound on the symbolic resonances of the name Matthew, which contrasts with how Matthew 16:18 hails Simon as the Πέτρος, or the foundational 'rock', of the 'assembly' (ἐκκλησία).[42]

While the theories above presuppose that the evangelist had a conscious literary or theological agenda for switching Levi for Matthew, Benjamin Bacon raised the possibility that the evangelist made an inadvertent error. In Bacon's reconstruction, Matthew 10:2–4 was based on a pre-Matthean list that a scribe was harmonizing with Mark 3:16–19. This copyist who transcribed the list of the twelve apostles also had access to a copy of Mark's Gospel with the alternate reading 'James the son of Alphaeus' rather than Levi at Mark 2:14[43] and, thus, inserted the note ὁ τελώνης in the margins between the names of Matthew and James in the list. The note ὁ τελώνης was originally meant to be applied to James, but the evangelist misunderstood it in reference to Matthew and changed Matthew 9:9 accordingly.[44] For Bacon's theory to work, he must take two huge, *a priori* assumptions for granted. The first assumption is that the evangelist received a list of the apostles where the name Matthew immediately preceded that of James, rather than editing the list from Mark 3:16–19 including changing the order of Matthew and Thomas, and the second is that the textual variant in Mark 2:14 which only surfaces in a handful of manuscripts (D Θ f^{13} 565 it) was older than the publication of Matthew's Gospel.[45]

---

36 Pesch, 'Levi-Matthäus', 56.
37 Beare, *The Gospel According to Matthew*, 225; Meier, *The Vision of Matthew*, 24-25.
38 Meier, *The Vision of Matthew*, 25 n.26.
39 Luz, *Matthew 8–20*, 32.
40 Kiley, 'Why "Matthew"', 348; cf. Carter, *Matthew*, 23–24.
41 Kiley, 'Why "Matthew"', 349–351.
42 Pesch, 'Levi-Matthäus', 47; Luz, *Matthew 8–20*, 32 n.13, n.21.
43 Lindars, 'Matthew, Levi, Lebbaeus', 222, is surely correct that this minority reading was motived by the 'scribe's desire for uniformity' by only having a single 'son of Alphaeus' in the text of Mark.
44 Bacon, *Studies in Matthew*, 39–40.
45 Pesch, 'Levi-Matthäus', 47–49; Kiley, 'Why "Matthew"', 348.

After reviewing these rival theories, I agree with Ulrich Luz that the most 'probable supposition is that it was still known of Matthew that he was a tax collector; therefore the story of Levi's call fits his situation'.[46] Levi's instant, positive response to Jesus's invitation to leave everything behind and follow him in Mark 2:14, like the call of the four fisherman in Mark 1:16–20, is brief and highly stylized. In light of this, Bauckham points out that the episode in Mark 2:14 could be applicable to any former tax gatherer who was invited by Jesus to join his movement in the world of the narrative.[47] Bauckham may make too much of the omission of the possessive pronoun αὐτοῦ ('his') after 'the house' in Matthew 9:15 (contra Mark 2:15) as showing that the evangelist only wished to appropriate Levi's call narrative for Matthew and not advance an unhistorical claim that Jesus was staying at Matthew's house in Capernaum.[48] It may be equally plausible that the evangelist omitted the pronoun because the referent in Mark 2:15 was ambiguous with regards to whether Levi or Jesus owned the house. Discounting this last argument, Luz and Bauckham still provide a satisfactory explanation for why Mark 2:14 was revised in Matthew 9:9 and turned into the scene of Matthew's transformative encounter with Jesus, because there was a vague recollection that Matthew had been a toll collector but the details of his employment and the time when or place where he had met Jesus had long been forgotten. The main weakness to their theory is that there is an absence of early and independent witnesses to corroborate that Matthew had been a toll collector. Yet a strong argument in favour of their theory is that the identification of an apostle as a toll collector seems to counter the evangelist's tendency to paint 'toll collectors' (τελῶναι) in an extremely unflattering light, suggesting that the evangelist had to deal with an inherited tradition about Matthew's occupation and did not invent it *ex nihilo*.[49]

The evangelist's disapproval of toll collectors in general can be observed in the pairing of them with 'sinners' (ἁμαρτωλοί; cf. 9:10–11; 11:19), 'Gentiles' (ἐθνικοί; cf. 5:46–47, 18:17), and 'prostitutes' (πόρναι; cf. 21:31–32). Granted, the evangelist repeated triple tradition (Mark 2:14–17/Matt 9:9–12, 13b/Luke 5:27–32) and double tradition (Matt 11:19/Luke 7:34) material about Jesus's ministry to 'toll collectors and sinners' (τελῶναι καὶ ἁμαρτωλοί). On the other hand, Matthew 5:46 reminds the readers that it is not commendable to love those who love them, for this is the bare minimum that even 'toll collectors' could achieve. In Matthew 18:17, a member of the Christ 'assembly' (ἐκκλησία) who was excommunicated is to be regarded as an outsider to this Jewish community like a 'toll collector' or a 'Gentile'. Finally, Matthew 21:31–32 (cf. Luke 3:12–13; 7:29–30) shames the chief priests by expressing how the socially despised 'toll collectors' and 'prostitutes' were admitted into God's kingdom ahead of them solely because 'they believed in' (ἐπιστεύσατε) the Baptizer's message of repentance. There is nothing like the parable in Luke 18:9–14 where a toll collector is declared to be in right standing with God after a penitential prayer, despite not changing his way of life.

---

46 Luz, *Matthew 8–20*, 32.
47 Bauckham, *Eyewitnesses*, 111.
48 Bauckham, *Eyewitnesses*, 111.
49 It is true that the 'criteria of authenticity' in historical Jesus research have been problematized in recent scholarship and Rafael Rodriguez, 'The Embarrassing Truth about Jesus', 132–51, contends that the criterion of embarrassment is impossible to apply as every pericope was preserved by some followers of Jesus to advance their interests. At the very least, though, scholars may be able to detect material that is incongruent with the wider themes of a particular Gospel that are identifiable through literary analysis. For example, it may be presumptuous to assume that all Christ followers were 'embarrassed' by John's baptism of Jesus, but the author of Matthew 3:13–17 clearly inherited the account of the baptism from a prior source (i.e. Mark 1:9–11) and attempted to do apologetic damage control by adding the conversation between John and Jesus in Matthew 3:14–15.

Based partly on the verses adduced above,[50] William O. Walker dissents from the widespread scholarly consensus that the historical Jesus had table fellowship with toll collectors (cf. Mark 2:14–17 par; Matt 11:19/Luke 7:34; Luke 19:1–10).[51] Of course, contrary to Walker, Jesus could have judged toll collectors to be sinful and 'sick' (cf. Mark 2:17 par), while still associating with them in the hope that they might repent of their actions. What should be noted is that the harsh attitude towards toll collectors is a characteristic feature of Matthew's *Sondergut*. This may not prove that these verses are redactional, rather than taken from sources that are no longer extant. For instance, Matthew 18:17 could be traditional or redactional.[52] Similarly, the parallel saying to Matthew 5:46 in Luke 6:32 only speaks about 'sinners' (ἁμαρτωλοί), so there is room for specialists on the Synoptic Problem to debate whether the Matthean or the Lukan saying is more faithful to the wording of Q or whether Luke edited Matthew's text.[53] Even if we could isolate Matthew's original contributions or editorial amendments with precision, it may be methodologically problematic to privilege redactional changes over preserved traditions, for the evangelist was a creative author who had command over all the material at his or her disposal and sought to communicate a unified, coherent story.[54] Regardless, in light of Matthew's whole story, toll collectors are portrayed as outsiders to and negative foils for the community that Jesus established (5:46; 18:17), unless they turn away from this way of life (9:12–13; 21:31–32).

Therefore, what distinguished the Apostle Matthew from the rest of the sinful toll collectors is that he fully abandoned his notorious profession at Jesus's call, for the evangelist could not tolerate a toll collector who continued to practice his trade after being summoned by Jesus to a life of discipleship. Since the exact details of Matthew's change in character were no longer remembered, the evangelist edited the Markan pericope about Levi, the son of Alphaeus, so that it now testified to the dramatic transformation of Matthew's vocation from a toll collector to an apostle. Matthew thus served as a pre-eminent example for Christian readers who had also undergone their own personal transformations. Yet it was later church authorities who built an elaborate construction of Matthean authorship on the tiny foundation of Matthew 9:9 and 10:3.

---

50 Walker, 'Jesus and the Tax Collectors', 224–27.
51 Walker, 'Jesus and the Tax Collectors', 221–238.
52 For instance, these three different options about the origins of Matthew 18:15–17 have been proposed in the redaction-critical commentaries. Luz, *Matthew 8–20*, 448–50, conjectures that the double tradition (Matt 18:15/Luke 17:3) had been expanded with the addition of a church rule from a Jewish Christ assembly prior to the composition of Matthew's Gospel. Davies & Allison, *Matthew VIII–XVIII*, 781, insist that verses 15–17 could have been found in the version of Q available to Matthew. Gundry, *Matthew*, 367–68, classifies verses 16–17 as redactional and detects signs of Matthean composition in them as well as in parts of verse 15 (cf. Luke 17:3).
53 For instance, both Davies & Allison, *Matthew I–VII*, 557–58, and Luz, *Matthew 1–7*, 345, suggest that Luke 6:32 substituted the general expression 'sinners' for Matthew's 'toll collectors'. In contrast, Gundry, *Matthew*, 99, writes, 'Luke's sinners have become tax collectors in agreement with Matthew's special attention to tax collectors, whom he interpolates three times and writes about twice in unique passages'.
54 For this point championed by narrative or literary critics, see Tolbert, *Sowing the Gospel*, 38.

Bibliography

Albright, W.F., & C.S. Mann — *Matthew* (AB; Doubleday: New York, 1971).

Bacon, B. — *Studies in Matthew* (New York: Henry Holt and Company, 1930).

Bauckham, R. — *Jesus and the Eyewitnesses: The Gospels as Eyewitness Testimony* (2nd ed.; Grand Rapids: Eerdmans, 2017).

Beare, F.W. — *The Gospel According to Matthew* (Cambridge: Harper & Row, 1981).

Black, M. — 'The Use of Rhetorical Terminology in Papias on Matthew and Mark', *Journal for the Study of the New Testament* 37 (1989), 31–41.

Blomberg, C.L. — *Matthew* (NAC; Nashville: Broadman, 1992).

Bond, H. — 'Was Peter Behind Mark's Gospel', in Helen Bond & Larry W. Hurtado (eds.), *Peter in Early Christianity* (Grand Rapids: Eerdmans, 2015), 46–61.

Boxall, I. — *Matthew through the Centuries* (Hoboken: Wiley Blackwell, 2019).

Brown, J.K., & K. Roberts — *Matthew* (Two Horizons; Grand Rapids: Eerdmans, 2018).

Cadbury, H.J. — *The Style and Literary Method of Luke and Acts* (Cambridge, Mass.: Harvard University Press, 1920).

Carson, D.A. — *Matthew: Chapters 1 through 12* (EBC; Grand Rapids: Zondervan, 1995).

Carter, W. — *Matthew: Storyteller, Interpreter, Evangelist* (Peabody: Hendrickson, 2004).

Davies, W.D., & D.C. Allison — *A Critical and Exegetical Commentary on The Gospel According to Saint Matthew. Volume I: Introduction and Commentary on Matthew I–VII* (ICC; Edinburgh: T&T Clark, 1988).

Davies, W.D., & D.C. Allison — *A Critical and Exegetical Commentary on The Gospel According to Saint Matthew. Volume II: Introduction and Commentary on Matthew VIII–XVII* (ICC; Edinburgh: T&T Clark, 1991).

Donahue, J.R. — 'Tax Collectors and Sinners: An Attempt at Identification', *Catholic Biblical Quarterly* 33 (1971), 36–61.

Edwards, J.R. — *The Hebrew Gospel and the Development of the Synoptic Tradition* (Grand Rapids: Eerdmans, 2009).

Ehrman, B. — *Forgery and Counterforgery: The Use of Literary Deceit in Early Christian Polemics* (Oxford: Oxford University Press, 2013).

France, R.T. — *Matthew: Evangelist and Teacher* (Grand Rapids: Zondervan, 1989).

Gnilka, J. — *Das Matthäusevangelium* (HTKNT; Freiburg: Herder, 1986).

Grant, F.C. — *The Gospels: Their Origins and Growth* (New York: Harper, 1957).

Gundry, R.H. — *The Use of the Old Testament in St. Matthew's Gospel: With Special Reference to the Messianic Hope* (Leiden: Brill, 1975).

Gundry, R.H.	*Matthew: A Commentary on his Handbook for a Mixed Church under Persecution* (2nd ed.; Grand Rapids: Eerdmans, 1994).
Hagner, D.A.	*Matthew 1–13* (Dallas: Word, 1993).
Hill, D.	*The Gospel of Matthew* (Grand Rapids: Eerdmans, 1972).
Hobart, W.K.	*The Medical Language of St Luke. A proof from internal evidence that "The Gospel according to St. Luke" and "The acts of the apostles" were written by the same person, and that the writer was a medical man* (Dublin: Dublin : Hodges, Figgis, & co, 1882).
Ilan, T.	*Lexicon of Jewish Names in Late Antiquity: Part I: Palestine 330 BCE – 200 CE* (TSAJ 91; Tübingen: Mohr Siebeck, 2002).
Keener, C.S.	*A Commentary on the Gospel of Matthew* (Grand Rapids: Eerdmans, 1999).
Kiley, M.	'Why "Matthew" in Matt 9:9–13', *Biblica* 65.3 (1984), 347–351.
Kilpatrick, G.D.	*The Origins of the Gospel according to St. Matthew* (Oxford: Clarendon, 1946).
Kok, M.J.	*The Gospel on the Margins: The Reception of Mark in the Second Century* (Minneapolis: Fortress, 2015).
Kok, M.J.	'Did Papias of Hierapolis Use the *Gospel according to the Hebrews* as a Source?', *JECS* 25.1 (2017), 29–53.
Lane, W.L.	*The Gospel of Mark* (NICNT; Grand Rapids: Eerdmans, 1974).
Lindars, B.	'Matthew, Levi, Lebbaeus and the Value of the Western Text', *New Testament Studies* 4 (1957–58), 220–222.
Luz, U.	*Matthew 1–7* (James E. Crouch, trans.; Hermeneia; Minneapolis: Fortress, 2007).
Luz, U.	*Matthew 8–20* (James E. Crouch, trans.; Hermeneia; Minneapolis: Fortress, 2001).
MacDonald, D.	*Two Shipwrecked Gospels: The Logoi of Jesus and Papias's Exposition of Logia about the Lord* (Atlanta: SBL, 2012).
Manson, T.W.	*Studies in the Gospels and Epistles* (Manchester: Manchester University Press, 1962).
Meier, J.P.	*The Vision of Matthew: Christ, Church and Morality in the First Gospel* (New York: Paulist, 1978).
Morris, L.L.	*The Gospel according to Matthew* (Grand Rapids: Eerdmans, 1992).
Mounce, R.H.	*Matthew* (NIBC; Peabody: Hendrickson, 1985).
Nolland, J.	*The Gospel of Matthew* (NIGTC; Grand Rapids: Eerdmans, 2005).
Osborne, G.R.	*Matthew* (ECNT; Grand Rapids: Zondervan, 2010).

Pesch, R.	'Levi-Matthäus (Mc 2.14/Mt 9.9; 10.3). Ein Beitrag zur Lösung eines alten Problems', *Zeitschrift für die neutestamentliche Wissenschaft* 59 (1968), 40–56.
Powers, B.W.	*The Progressive Publication of Matthew: An Explanation of the Writing of the Synoptic Gospels* (Nashville: B&H Publishing Group, 2010).
Rendel, H.J.	'The "Logia" and the Gospels', *Contemporary Review* 72 (1897), 341–348.
Rodriguez, R.	'The Embarrassing Truth about Jesus: The Criterion of Embarrassment and the Failure of Historical Authenticity', in Chris Keith & Anthony Le Donne (eds.), *Jesus, Criteria, and the Demise of Authenticity* (London and New York: T&T Clark, 2012), 132–151.
Schleiermacher, F.	'Über die Zeugnisse des Papias von unsern beiden ersten Evangelien', *Theologische Studien und Kritiken* 5 (1832), 735–68.
Simonetti, M.	*Matthew 1—13* (ACCS New Testament 1a; Downers Grove: IVP, 2001).
Tolbert, M.A.	*Sowing the Gospel: Mark's World in Literary-Historical Perspective* (Minneapolis: Fortress, 1989).
Walker, W.	'Jesus and the Tax Collectors', *Journal of Biblical Literature* 97 (1978), 221–238.
Witherington, B., III	*Matthew* (Macon: Smyth & Helywys, 2006).

Michael J. Kok
Vose Seminary, an affiliate of the Australian College of Theology
Michael.Kok@vose.edu.au

A Certain Wisdom in Nazareth (Mark 6:2b)

PETER G. BOLT

Abstract

Although it is usual to render the Nazarene's response to Jesus (Mark 6:2b) as three questions, it consists of only one, which is a three-part question about the origin of Jesus' wisdom and miracles. The first part is the question proper, asking after the source of 'these thigs' (ταῦτα). The second and third part consist of two phrases which together explicate the demonstrative pronoun with a 'both ... and ...' (καὶ ... καὶ ...) construction. Instead of accenting τίς in the second part, it should be read as the unaccented indefinite pronoun, indicating that the Nazarenes viewed Jesus as having 'a certain wisdom', which they view negatively. It is likely that they had adopted a similar position to that of the scribes from Jerusalem, that Jesus' words and deeds were not from God, but from the underworld powers.

1. A Certain Wisdom in Nazareth

After Jesus' hometown synagogue (i.e. in Nazareth, see Mark 1:9,24) was astounded at his teaching, they began to ask questions about their well-known visitor. According to Mark, they asked (6:2):

> Πόθεν τούτῳ ταῦτα, καὶ τίς ἡ σοφία ἡ δοθεῖσα τούτῳ, καὶ αἱ δυνάμεις τοιαῦται διὰ τῶν χειρῶν αὐτοῦ γινόμεναι;

Translators and commentators alike find three questions here, with two more to come in verse 3. Along with this clear enumeration, however, comes an awkward syntax of which the commentators complain and which the translators seek to overcome.

The awkward syntax arises because the Greek does not have a verb in any of the three parts of the Nazarenes' questioning. The verb 'to be' (ἐστιν) is correctly understood and supplied by translators after the interrogative πόθεν.[1] By reading the τίς as an interrogative (accented), the words after the first καί can also be rendered into a complete sentence by supplying ἐστιν, but after the second καί, with no interrogative and being an articular participle phrase, this is impossible. There is no easy way to render the final part into a complete sentence (question) as it stands.

---

1 'Adverb', BDF #104; 'pronominal adjective', Goodwin, *Greek Grammar* #436.

A CERTAIN WISDOM IN NAZARETH (MARK 6:2B)

1.1 The English Translations

The difficulty is evident in the different renderings of the second and the final parts found in the standard English translations (*italics* original; underlining showing variation):

> What wisdom *is* this which is given unto him, that even such mighty works are wrought by his hands? (KJV)

> What wisdom *is* this which is given to Him, that such mighty works are performed by His hands! (NKJV)

> What is the wisdom that is given unto this man, and *what mean* such mighty works wrought by his hands? (ASV)

> What is *this* wisdom given to Him, and such miracles as these performed by His hands? (NASB 95)

> What is this wisdom that has been given to him? What deeds of power are being done by his hands! (NRSV)

> What is the wisdom given to him? How are such mighty works done by his hands? (ESV)

> What's this wisdom that has been given him? What are these remarkable miracles he is performing? (NIV 2011)

> What is this wisdom given to Him, and how are these miracles performed by His hands? (HCSB)

> What is this wisdom that has been given to him, and how are these miracles performed by his hands? (CSB 2017)

After what is clearly a question (πόθεν τούτῳ ταῦτα) in the first part of the Nazarenes' speech, each of these versions reads τίς as an interrogative and supplies a form of 'to be' in order to render the second part as a further question. Consistent with this treatment of the second part, most English versions also punctuate the third part as a question (KJV, ASV, NASB, ESV, NIV, HCSB, CSB), although—no doubt arising from the Nazarenes' astonishment (v.2a) and from the force of τοιαῦται—some punctuate the third as an exclamation (NKJV, NRSV). Although the only verbal form in the third and final part is the participle γινόμεναι, this tends to be rendered as an indicative by all but the ASV/NASB, despite the fact that the existence of such an 'independent participle' standing for the indicative is a matter of dispute among grammarians, and, in any case, even if occasionally present in the New Testament under Semitic influence,[2] it is certainly not Greek.[3] In addition, all of the selected translations paraphrase rather than translate γινόμεναι— despite the existence of several Greek words that could have been selected in the original if

---

[2] So Moule, *Idiom Book*, 31, 179, in regards to participles standing for imperatives and indicatives and citing Rom 5:11; 12:9ff; Phil 3:4; 2 Cor 5:12; 7:5; 8:4; 9:11,13. The Semitic idiom in question may be where a construction begun by a finite verb is continued by a series of co-ordinated participles (see BDF #468), which, in any case, does not pertain in Mark 6:2. Cf. Kautzsch, *Gesenius' Hebrew Grammar*, 357.

[3] 'There may also be examples of a participle being used independently as an indicative. The matter is disputed by grammarians. Much depends upon whether one supplies an anacoluthon or treats the participle as it stands in the sentence. Certainly no participle should be explained as an independent participle if there is another way to explain it'; Brooks & Winbery, *Syntax*, 152. Wallace, *Greek Grammar*, 653, concurs. Moule, *Idiom Book*, 179, also notes, however, that W. Bauer, *Apost. Väter*, claims some evidence for the usage in pre-Christian κοιν. I have been unable to examine this evidence.

'performed' or 'wrought' or 'done' was what was required (e.g. ποιέω cf. 6:5, 9:39; ἐνεργέω, 6:14; or even ἐργάζομαι, cf. Luke 13:14; John 9:4). Continuing the struggle to provide better English sense, other supplements are added, whether 'that' (KJV, NKJV), 'what mean' (ASV), 'how' (ESV, HCSB, CSB), or 'what are' (NIV). In addition, while the καί that marks off this final section is rendered as 'and' by ASV, NASB, HCSB, CSB, or the emphatic 'even' by the KJV, it is ignored by the NKJV, NRSV, ESV, and NIV.

But it is not new to find awkwardness in the Nazarenes' syntax. The textual tradition indicates that ancient copyists had already felt the need to improve what they found in their exemplar.

1.2 The Textual Tradition

UBS 5 supplies the following text for verse 2b:

καὶ πολλοὶ ἀκούοντες ἐξεπλήσσοντο λέγοντες, Πόθεν τούτῳ ταῦτα, καὶ τίς ἡ σοφία ἡ δοθεῖσα τούτῳ, καὶ αἱ δυνάμεις τοιαῦται διὰ τῶν χειρῶν αὐτοῦ γινόμεναι;

The textual tradition can be grouped into five (sets of) variants of the final part of the questioning, that is, the words found after its second καί.

a) καὶ αἱ δυνάμεις … γινόμεναι ℵ* B (L 579 ℓ 890 *omit* αἱ) 892 1342 cop^{bo} geo

UBS 5 prints this as a 'C' reading, namely, one 'that the Committee had difficulty in deciding which variant to place in the text'.[4] In the *Textual Commentary*, Metzger explains that:

> A majority of the Committee preferred the grammatically difficult reading of the Alexandrian text (ℵ* B 33 892 *al*) as best accounting for the origin of the other readings; thus, some witnesses added αἱ after τοιαῦται (ℵ^c L Δ), while many others eliminated the article before δυνάμεις and changed the participle into a finite verb, either γίνονται or γίνωνται (introduced by ἵνα). The latest reading, which was incorporated into the Textus Receptus, prefixes ὅτι to the indicative clause.[5]

b) καὶ αἱ δυνάμεις αἱ τοιαῦται αἱ … γινόμεναι ℵ¹ Δ 33^{vid}

By adding an article prior to τοιαῦται and another article to govern the participle and enclose the prepositional phrase, this reading simply clarifies the reading accepted by UBS 5, ie. it clarifies the fact that all the words after the second καί, from the prepositional phrase to the participle, are the one articular participle phrase, without trying to turn them into a finite sentence.

c) ἵνα καὶ δυνάμεις … γίνωνται C*D (Θ 700 *omit* καί) 180 597 ℓ 68 ℓ 637 ℓ 813 ℓ 1223 it^{(b), d, ff2} (it^{i, q, r1} syr^p *omit* καί) syr^{h, (pal)} arm TOB

By adding ἵνα and modifying the participle γινόμεναι to a subjunctive γίνωνται, this reading seeks to subordinate the words after the second καί to those after the first καί. Presumably the copyists behind this reading have read τίς in the second part as the interrogative and also supplied 'to be' in order to make a complete sentence. Consistent with their change to the subjunctive, the article before δυνάμεις is also omitted, generalizing the powers. Some manuscripts then smooth things further by omitting the second καί altogether, which would otherwise need to be emphatic.

---

4   UBS 5, p.8*.
5   Metzger, *Textual Commentary*, 75.

d) καὶ δυνάμεις … γίνονται A C2 W f¹ f¹³ (28 828 δυνάμεις τοιαῦται) 157 205 565 1006 1010 1071 (1241 αἱ δυνάμεις) (1243 δυνάμεις τοσαῦται) 1424 1505 Byz [E F G H (Ν Σ αἱ δυνάμεις)] Lect it[a, aur, c, e, l] vg slav

The change of the participle γινόμεναι to the present indicative γίνονται creates a proper sentence, with most manuscripts adopting this reading also dropping the article before δυνάμεις, generalizing the powers, and turning the sentence into an emphatic statement, presumably making the powers consequential on the wisdom given him.

e) ὅτι καὶ δυνάμεις … γίνονται 1292 (it[f] omit καί)

By supplying ὅτι to the previous set of variants (d), this reading clarifies what is presumed by it, namely, that the existence of the powers are consequential on the wisdom. Both these last two readings therefore conform the question materially to what happened in the Capernaum synagogue (1:21–28), whereby the authority heard in the teaching was backed up by the miraculous display in the exorcism.

1.3 A Certain (Kind of) Wisdom

Although Luke has no parallel to the expression (cf. Luke 4:22), Matthew 13:54 has it an abbreviated form.

Πόθεν τούτῳ   ἡ σοφία   αὕτη
        καὶ   αἱ δυνάμεις;

Assuming Markan priority, Matthew drops Mark's more expansive—and 'problematic'— portions, adding a demonstrative to the first substantive (arguably, prompted by Mark's ταῦτα). Clearly Matthew has read a singular question about the origin of 'this' wisdom and the associated miracles, pure and simple.

Historically speaking, that the Jews were concerned with the source of Jesus' teaching can be confirmed by the same simple question expressed in another form recorded in John 7:15—which, significantly, is set in a context which parallels that of Mark 6:

ἐθαύμαζον οὖν οἱ Ἰουδαῖοι λέγοντες, Πῶς οὗτος γράμματα οἶδεν μὴ μεμαθηκώς;

So the Jews were marveling, saying, 'How does this one know letters, not being learned?'

The similarity of structure between Matthew's simpler version and Mark's more extended version is easily discernible—for the moment leaving aside τίς and τοιαῦται (here marked by the ellipses), which will be dealt with below:

Πόθεν τούτῳ   ταῦτα,
        καὶ   […] ἡ σοφία   ἡ δοθεῖσα   τούτῳ,
        καὶ   αἱ δυνάμεις […]   διὰ τῶν χειρῶν αὐτοῦ γινόμεναι;

To work back from the common ground with Matthew, clearly Mark also deals with the two aspects of Jesus' ministry portrayed to this point in his narrative: his word (part 2) and his deed (part 3). Each is given in an expanded version, and each phrase makes perfect sense as a descriptive phrase without any need to supply a verb in an attempt to turn it into a clause: 'the wisdom given to this man'; 'the powers coming about through his hands'. Thus, what is usually considered to be three questions is actually only one.

To open the question (part 1), the Nazarenes begin with a generality, referring to these two dimensions by means of the plural demonstrative pronoun ταῦτα referring to them both: they want to know the origin of 'these things'. As the structure shows, without inserting any further interrogative or supplying any verb to create any clauses, the two instances of καί can be taken as providing a further elaboration of the demonstrative pronoun (the subject of the question Πόθεν τούτῳ ..., 'from whence to this man [are] ...') by providing two descriptive phrases (not clauses) connected together in a καί ... καί ..., 'both ... and ...', construction. By focusing firstly on his 'words' and then on his 'deeds', the Nazarenes utilise the usual categories used in the ancient world to sum up a person's character (cf. Luke 24:19; Acts 7:22; Rom 15:18; 2 Cor 10:11; Col 3:17; 2 Thess 2:17; 1 John 3:18).[6] For readers of Mark, this accords with the congruence between his words and deeds that has already been depicted in the preceding narrative (1:21–28; 1:40–45; 2:1–12; cf. 3:14–15).

To complete the picture, the two words left to one side thus far, τίς, or—as it would appear in an unaccented manuscript—τις, and τοιαῦται, need to be reinserted, for each qualifies their phrase significantly:

Πόθεν τούτῳ ταῦτα,
    καὶ   **τις** ἡ σοφία   ἡ δοθεῖσα   τούτῳ,
    καὶ   αἱ δυνάμεις **τοιαῦται**   διὰ τῶν χειρῶν αὐτοῦ γινόμεναι;

What has astonished the synagogue gathering in Jesus' hometown, as it did the Capernaum synagogue earlier in Mark's account (1:21–28), is the extraordinary character of both his 'word and deed'.

On the one hand, this is particularly brought out by their use of τοιαῦται, 'such (kind of)', which speaks not so much of the number of his miracles (which was extraordinary enough), but of their quality, or nature, or kind. For the Nazarenes, this refers to what they have heard rumoured abroad about Jesus' activity around the Sea of Galilee, or more particularly, in Capernaum (Mark 1:21–28; 1:29–34; 2:1–12; 5:21–43; cf. Luke 4:23).[7] The reader of Mark's account naturally fills in the referent from the immediately preceding account climaxing with the raising of the synagogue ruler's daughter from the dead.[8] The extraordinary nature of 'such powers' naturally raises the question of their source. Where did 'such powers' come from?

However, and on the other hand, what about the qualification given to the phrase about Jesus' word? The point of mentioning the *unaccented* τις is because it opens up another possibility, not usually considered. For rather than being an interrogative, the unaccented τις is an indefinite pronoun, whether masculine or feminine. Here it would be feminine, acting as an adjectival

---

6 For literature, note the passing comment by Blundell, *The Play of Character*, 49, about '... the matching of word and deed (*logos* and *ergon*) with which ancient Greek texts are almost obsessively preoccupied', and further pp.80, 130–31. For an example of the 'word and deed' motif in the inscriptional evidence, see Harrison, *Paul and the Ancient Celebrity* Circuit, 149–150, 194–196, 273, 308, for various reflections on *IEph* Ia 6: II cent. AD, which provided guidance for young men in the gymnasium (NB line 19: 'the reputation of the young men being fostered both in word and deed [καὶ λόγωι καὶ ἔργωι]'). Harrison notes that 'the combination of noble actions with finesse in words point to the holistic character transformation expected not only of benefactors but also in the people that they mentor' (p.273).
7 Mark depicts the news of Jesus spreading in increasingly broader circles, with the crowd in 3:7–12 arriving (in response) from vast distances.
8 So also Guelich, *Mark*, 309. Each of the suppliants with whom Jesus has dealt thus far in the narrative stand in some kind of relationship with death and Jesus' interventions are therefore him dealing with death as a foretaste of his coming resurrection from the dead; see the relevant sections in my *Jesus' Defeat of Death*.

modifier of ἡ σοφία, and to be translated 'a certain (kind of) wisdom'.[9]

What is the significance of this addition? At the least, it provides a rider to the 'wisdom' by hinting towards some kind of unarticulated qualification, indicating that although some may see it as 'wisdom', the synagogue crowd might not recognise it as such. As in other usages of τις, this then opens up the possibility that the speaker is adding a nuance of contempt for this kind of 'so-called wisdom'.[10] In the context of the Nazareth synagogue this becomes understandable as the pericope proceeds to show that the crowd thought they knew Jesus' family of origin too well to allow him to stand out from the ordinary crowd. They were 'scandalized' by him (v. 3b), and Jesus, in turn, was amazed at their lack of faith (v.6).

But there must be more to their lack of faith than simply seeing him as too ordinary. After all, they were aware of the wisdom and miracles that had impressed others sufficiently enough to draw huge crowds, and they do not appear to have denied the reality of either of these things. His ordinary origins do not negate the fact that 'these things' were manifest in him. Their question was in regard to the source of his notable words and extraordinary deeds.

As with Jesus' later question to the chief priests, scribes and elders, the synagogue crowd would be interested to know if his word and deed indicated that he was ἐξ οὐρανοῦ 'from Heaven', or ἐξ ἀνθρώπων 'of human origin' (cf. 11:30). There is a 'certain wisdom' that would be human wisdom as opposed to that of God (cf. 8:33)—a wisdom in one's own eyes, in contrast to that beginning with the fear of YHWH (Prov 3:7).[11]

But 'powers such as these' do not speak of merely human actions. No mere human being could have raised the dead. If his miracles were not 'from God', then another option presented itself and it had already been named by the scribes who had come down from Jerusalem (3:22). These men attributed his miracles to the power of an unclean spirit, Beelzeboul, the prince of demons, whom Jesus (and, by implication of the conversation, his opponents)[12] evidently equated with Satan (3:22,26,30). Because 'the prince of demons' would be understood to refer to the one in charge of the underworld who could release the powers of the dead for the use of magicians,[13] this charge was tantamount to accusing Jesus of magical action. As Mark's narrative proceeds, the readers will learn that this is the same belief that Herod Antipas had come to, specifically identifying the underworld spirit that had been 'raised' and was now being wielded as a weapon in Jesus' hands as the beheaded John the Baptist (6:14–16).[14]

---

9   See LSJ, s.v. A.; for the adjectival use, Wallace, *Greek Grammar*, 347. Mark has five other examples of this indefinite pronoun following immediately after καί, although in one instance it is pronominal (14:57) and in four instances it is modified by a partitive genitive (7:1; 8:3; 11:5; 15:35). Although Mark has no other instance of the adjectival use immediately after καί, Acts has several: **καί τις** ἀνήρ 'and a certain man' (Acts 3:2; 14:8), **καί τινας** ἄλλους 'and certain others' (15:2), **καί τις** γυνή 'and a certain woman' (16:14), **καί τινας** ἀδελφοὺς 'and certain brothers' (17:6), **καί τινας** ἑτέρους δεσμώτας 'and some other prisoners' (27:1).

10 See LSJ, s.v. A.II.3, 'in reference to a definite person, whom one wishes to avoid naming; [...] so also euphem. for something bad'; A.II.6a with proper names, 'one named so-and-so', with the nuance of contempt.

11 Fohrer, 'σοφία, σοφός', 487.

12 *Contra* Foerster, 'Βεεζεβούλ', 605, 'in His answer Jesus tacitly substitutes Satan', if this implies that he differed from his opponents on this point.

13 For cross-cultural analogies to this expression/being, see Bolt, *Jesus' Defeat of Death*, 123–128.

14 Bolt, *Jesus' Defeat of Death*, 191–192; noted also by Kraeling, 'Necromancy?'; Smith, *Magician*, 33f.; cf. Aune, 'Magic', 1541–1542.

2. A Certain Wisdom in Historical Perspective

Understanding the historical situation requires the piecing together of information in Mark's text with what is also known from other sources.

2.1 A Certain Wisdom

There was no doubt that Jesus had attracted fame because he spoke 'a certain wisdom', but what was its true nature? Whereas the other Synoptics (in Q material) have positive associations between Jesus and God's wisdom, this is the only occasion when Mark utilizes any words of the 'wisdom' family and, with the addition of τις, it is a wisdom under suspicion.

In biblical thought, wisdom can be viewed negatively or positively depending upon its source. That 'the Lord grants wisdom, from his mouth are knowledge and understanding' (Prov 2:6)[15] is axiomatic in OT thought, from the practical skill of Bezalel, Oholiab, and others in knowing how to do the work required for the for the tabernacle (Exodus 36:1–2; cf. 35:31), to the world-renowned wisdom of Solomon (1 Kings 4:29–34). Possession of חכמה, 'wisdom', was not theoretical knowledge of the world, but practical control over it (Job 28:25–27).[16] Because wisdom is the practical mastery of the world, it is intimately related to power to live in the world.[17] As the ability to master the environment,[18] it is only a short step to the magicians' wisdom that seeks to manipulate the world for their own antisocial purposes.

In Israel's wider environment the language of wisdom was also associated with magical skill.[19] Ancient Israel was well acquainted with the wisdom of the Babylonians (Jer 50:35; 51:57; cf. Isa 44:25; 47:10) and Egyptians (1 Kings 4:30; cf. Gen 41:8; Exod 7:11), as well as that associated with their closer neighbours (Canaanites, Ezek 28:3,17; Phoenicians, Ezek 27:8; Zech. 9:2; Edomites, Jer 49:7; Ob 8; Job 2:11), all of which was tainted with a magical connection.[20] The wise men of Babylon and Egypt and Persia were associated with the magical arts (Gen 41:8; Exod 7:11; Isa 44:25; 47:10, cf. v. 9, 12; Dan 2:27; 4:3; Esther 1:13, cf. the *magi* of Matt 2:1).[21] There were notable clashes between the 'wise men/magicians' of Egypt and Babylon, in the stories of Joseph and Daniel. The wisdom of the magician was forbidden, not because it didn't work, but because the people of God should turn to God and his word instead (Isa 8:19–22). The clash was about origins: whether wisdom was from God, or whether it was not.

With this 'negative' wisdom constantly in the background, even though Solomon's great wisdom was clearly given to him by God (1 Kings 3; 4:29–34), this did not prevent it from falling under the suspicion of magical power—even with the insistence that his magic was beneficent,

---

15   Wilckens, 'σοφία, σοφός', 506–507.
16   Fohrer, 'σοφία, σοφός', 489–490, 492.
17   Wilckens, 'σοφία, σοφός', 514–515. nn.25–26, noting, for σοφία and δύναμις together, 1 Cor 1:24; cf. Matt 7:22; Acts 6:8; 2 Cor 12:12; the association of λόγος ἀληθείας and δύναμις θεοῦ in 2 Cor 6:7; and also λόγος σοφίας in 1 Cor 12:8 and ἐνεργήματα δυνάμεων in 12:10, cf. also Acts 4:33.
18   Fohrer, 'σοφία, σοφός', 480.
19   Fohrer, 'σοφία, σοφός', 477–478.
20   Fohrer, 'σοφία, σοφός', 480.
21   Fohrer, 'σοφία, σοφός', 483–484. For the *magi*, see McCasland, 'Magi'.

not maleficent.[22] Solomon's wisdom gave him a long currency in magical circles and the belief that he had such power may even lie behind the instances in the Gospels where Jesus is addressed as 'son of David' in exorcism/healing contexts (Mark 10:47,48; but also note 12:35,37).[23]

Jesus' teaching was after the style of the teacher of wisdom, especially in his use of aphorisms, parables and riddles.[24] As with Daniel's wisdom, Jesus appeared to know the secrets about the future,[25] especially those related to the kingdom of God at the end of time (e.g. Mark 1:15; 4:26–29; 9:1; 13:7b,19; cf. Dan 2:30; 5:11,14; 12:1–13). The recognition of his teaching having authority, not as the scribes (1:22,27), is also a recognition of his wisdom, since wisdom as mastery of the world is also inevitably associated with power. For the same reason, his well-reputed ability to heal and to deal with underworld spirits also speaks of a powerful wisdom at work in him.

Given wisdom's significant ambiguity, for all concerned and especially for the Nazarenes, the ultimate issue was whether the widely-renowned wisdom of Jesus, was also —as his own brother, who was closely related to the discussion in the Nazareth synagogue, would later label it—that heavenly 'wisdom that comes from above' (ἡ ἄνωθεν σοφία) and so builds a peaceful society (cf. James 3:17–18), or that 'earthly, unspiritual, demonic' (ἐπίγειος, ψυχική, δαιμονιώδης) (so-called) wisdom that destroys it (James 3:14–16). Given that wisdom and power were not only attributes of God himself (e.g. Job 12:13), but also part of the eschatological blessing to be embodied in the coming Messiah (Isa 11:2; 33:5–6),[26] the stakes were high in getting this judgement wrong.[27]

2.2 A Certain *Prohibited* Wisdom

As the reports of 'Jesus of Nazareth' became more widely known, they not only attracted the attention of the crowds that came to him from far-flung regions (3:7–8), but they also attracted the attention of Herod Antipas (6:14–16) and the religious men from all over Galilee and, significantly, from Judea and Jerusalem (3:22; 7:1; cf. Luke 5:17).[28] When some 'scribes from Jerusalem'

---

22 For Solomon's reputation, with wisdom and beneficent power even surpassing the Egyptians, see Josephus, *Ant.* 8.45-47. For examples of the tradition that he operated magically, see *Testament of Solomon*, 11Q11 (or 11QapocrPs), later amulets and the magical papyri. For the latter magical texts, see McCown, 'Christian Tradition'. The Targum on Psalm 91 'reflects a very old tradition of Solomon as healer and exorcist par excellence', Evans, 'Jesus and Psalm 91', 548-549. Evans discusses much of the primary evidence for the tradition, both inside and outside Jewish circles. He also notes that 'there is abundant evidence of interest in Solomon, son of David, in the first century as exorcist par excellence' (p.552).
23 For Mark, see Charlesworth, 'Solomon and Jesus'. For an exploration of this possibility in Matthew's Gospel, see Duling, 'Solomon'.
24 Fohrer, 'σοφία, σοφός', 481.
25 Fohrer, 'σοφία, σοφός', 489. Cf. Pharr, 'Interdict', 280: 'Under the empire additional causes arose for the prohibition of magic. One of the claims of the magician was the ability to prophesy the future. When these prophecies presumed to say at what time and under what circumstances the ruling emperor would die, abdicate, or be overthrown, the result was politically unsettling, and harsh measures were taken from the time of Augustus to stamp out the practice'.
26 Fohrer, 'σοφία, σοφός', 488. It is also significant that Israel was to listen to the Prophet who is to Come (cf. Mark 9:7), in contrast to the magical arts (Deut 18:14-15).
27 It is interesting to read Mark 6:1-6 against the 'common wisdom myth lying behind various Jewish texts', especially those associated with Jewish Apocalyptic (EthEn 42) that wisdom descended from heaven and, after not finding acceptance, ascended again in resignation until she is found by those not seeking her. See Wilckens, 'σοφία, σοφός', 508-509, citing EthEn 94:5-6; cf. 98:3; 93:8; 4 Esr 5:9-10; S. Bar 48:33-36; and also Prov 1:20-33; Sir 24; Bar 3:9-4:4.
28 The scribes from Jerusalem might have been present in the dispute in 9:14, but this is not said and the presumption is therefore that they were local scribes, like the earlier scribes known to the people of Capernaum (1:22; 2:6). It is possible, of course, that Jerusalem scribes were present on other occasions even if not definitively identified as such.

arrived in Galilee (3:22; 7:1), this was almost certainly an official deputation sent to investigate the rumours—possibly after being called in by the local Pharisees[29]—similar to the delegations that were later sent to test Jesus (11:27–28; 12:13,18,28,34), or those, according to John, sent to investigate the Baptist (John 1:19,22,24) or to arrest Jesus (John 7:32,45). The rumours—if not the local Pharisees and Herodians—would have directed them to Capernaum, just as many others had flocked to this small town where so much had happened. However, since the subject of their inquiry was widely and well known as Jesus 'the Nazarene',[30] it is certainly possible that this appellative also led them to his home town, which would have enabled the members of this synagogue to have learned the 'official' version of Jesus' inspiration directly.

By the time the Jerusalem delegates visited Galilee, the local Pharisees had already taken council with the Herodians about the best way to ensure Jesus would be killed (3:6; cf. 12:13). Since the scribes were the biblical scholars of the Pharisees (2:16),[31] the arrival of the deputation of scribes from Jerusalem also brought the official evaluation of Jesus' ministry: he was practicing sorcery (3:22,30).[32] Herod Antipas had also come to this opinion, troubled as he was by the prospect of Jesus manipulating the ghost of John, who, as both βιαιοθάνατος 'one violently killed' and ἀκέφαλος 'a headless one', would be in a class much prized by the magicians for their vengeful power. So the two parties already plotting towards Jesus' untimely demise were also agreed about the source of his power.

Despite the frequent prohibitions of magical practices in the law (e.g. Exod 22:18; Lev 19:26,31; Deut 13:1–5; 18:10–15), reinforced in their breach throughout the rest of Israel's history (e.g.

---

29 So Black, 'Scribe', 248.

30 Rather than the more common Ναζωραῖος, Mark only uses Ναζαρηνός: 1:24; 10:47; 14:67, 16:6; cf. Luke 4:34 [= Mark 1:24]; 24:19 [L]. Cf. Ναζωραιος: Matt 2:23; 26:71; John 18:5,7; 19:19; Luke 18:37; Acts 2:22; 3:6; 4:10; 6:14; 22:8; 24:5; 26:9; cf. Ἰησοῦν τὸν ἀπὸ Ναζαρέθ: Matt 21:11; John 1:45; Acts 10:38. After assembling the texts, Schaeder, 'Ναζαρηνός, Ναζωραῖος', 4.874, comments: 'The passages adduced show that the two terms are not self-designations on the part of Jesus and His disciples, but that they were called this by the world around'. This is not the place to answer the various attempts to deny Nazareth its existence in Jesus' time, but Schaeder's comment is apt: 'One has only to think of the pains which Mt. and Lk. had to take to reconcile the fact that Jesus was a native of Nazareth with the birth in Bethlehem demanded by Micah 5:1. It is of little moment that there is no mention of Nazareth in Joseph. or Rabb. writings, and that the first ref. outside the NT is only in the 3rd cent. in Julius Africanus' (p.878). According to Julius Africanus (Eus., *HE* 1.7.14f), along with Cochaba ('village of the star', cf. Num 24:17), Nazareth was one of the villages named according to messianic hopes, namely, 'village of the branch' (Isa 11:1), whose residents were descendants of a non-royal line of the house of David, through Bathsheba's son, Nathan (2 Sam 5:14; 1 Chron 3:5; 14:4; Zech 12:12; Luke 3:31) and Zerubbabel, cherishing their connection with the messianic hope embedded in Isaiah's branch. For discussion, see Pixner, 'Paths', ch.1, 381–385; Bauckham, *Jude and the Relatives*, 60–70, ch.7.

31 There may have been scribes who were also Sadducees, but the argument is made on the rather thin evidence of the counter-inference from the expression 'scribes of the Pharisees' (Mark 2:16; Acts 23:9), and 'one inconclusive reference in Josephus (War 6.5.3) to ἱερογραμματεῖς, where the context appears to favour "priestly scribes"': Black, 'Scribe', 247. The deduction from Josephus also assumes that 'priestly' would be equated with 'Sadducee', which is not a foregone conclusion. Some priests were Sadduceean, but that does not mean all.

32 Those recognising that this was a charge of sorcery include Jeremias, *Central Message*, 41; McCasland, 'Magi', 221; Smith, *Magician*; Stanton, 'Jesus of Nazareth'; Welch, 'Law, Magic, Miracles'; Instone-Brewer, 'Jesus of Nazareth's Trial', 292. For further discussion, see the retrospective by Korsvoll, 'Jesus of Nazareth Revisited', which focuses on Geller and the Aramaic bowl incantations. For the continuation of the charge in later centuries, see Justin Martyr, *Dial.* 69.7; Origen, c.*Celsum* 1.6; Arnobius, *Adv.Nat.* 1.44; *b.Sanh.* 43a: '**On the eve of Passover they hung Yeshu the Notzri.** And the herald went out before him for forty days [saying]: "Yeshu the Notzri will go out to be stoned **for sorcery** and misleading **and enticing Israel** [to idolatry]"' (**bold** is the core tradition with the rest later glosses, as identified by Instone-Brewer, 'Jesus of Nazareth's Trial', 289); *b.Sanh.* 107b: 'And a Master has said, "Jesus the Nazarene practiced magic and led Israel astray"'; *Toledoth Yeshu* (9th c.) has Jesus healing by magical incantation.

1 Sam 28; 2 Kings 9:22; 21:6; 2 Chron 33:6; Isa 3:2–3; 8:19–20; Jer 27:9; Ezek 13:18–20),[33] Jews were renowned for their magical arts from ancient times, into the first century (A.D.), and beyond.[34] Because of the prohibitions of magical practices, the religious authorities were required to be able to discern the difference which meant that, even though in the NT period the 'scribe' was a technical term for a trained biblical scholar,[35] their own wisdom perhaps also included the knowledge of the secret arts.[36]

What basis would they have for charging Jesus with sorcery? Although it needed interpretation, the raw evidence was there alongside his words in his deeds. Even if interpreters ancient and modern have tried to distance his actions from those of the magicians by denying he used magical paraphernalia,[37] there were those amongst his contemporaries who gained a different impression. Some wanted to be healed by touching him —and they were healed by that touch (5:27–29; 6:56). Some saw him accomplish similar kinds of miracles using the same means as other magicians, such as touch (5:23; 6:5; 7:33; 8:23,25), perhaps oil (cf. 6:13), spittle (8:23), or, according to John, spittle, mud, and washing (John 9:11,14–15). Similarly, despite there being a marked simplicity in the words he used to bring about his acts of power compared to the lengthy and elaborate incantations on the lips of the magicians, to the raw observer of at least some of his miracles, his words of power nevertheless had a magical feel about them (5:41 Talitha koum!; 7:34 Ephphatha!). His popularity with the crowds could also speak against him. Although the beneficiaries of his powers might praise him for doing good and saving life (cf. Mark 3:4), the authorities were troubled by his flaunting of the traditions which, in their opinion, held the nation together (2:18–3:6; 7:1–23).[38] They were therefore disturbed by the growing crowds. According to Luke, they accused him before Pilate of, amongst other things, 'subverting our nation' (23:2a, διαστρέφοντα τὸ ἔθνος ἡμῶν), because 'he stirs up the people' (23:5, ἀνασείει τὸν λαόν), 'misleading the people' (23:14, ἀποστρέφοντα τὸν λαόν)—actions consistent with the antisocial nature of magic.

But perhaps the pre-eminent indicator of Jesus' sorcery was presented by his exorcisms, which displayed such clear power over the beings of the underworld, who were evidently quaking in his presence and silenced at his command (1:24,34; 3:11–12; 5:7–13). For a core part of the magicians' *modus operandi* was to generate fear in the underworld powers by threatening them with the names of higher and even more mighty and fearsome beings than they themselves were. In a sense, therefore, the scribes from Jerusalem gave indirect testimony to the nature of Jesus' miraculous deeds and to the power displayed in them, when they concluded that he must be operating by 'Beelzeboul, the Prince of the *daemones*' (3:22). Antipas, likewise, indirectly testifies to the exalted and extraordinary powers at work through Jesus' hands, by fearing that his source

---

33 Cf. Mendelsohn, 'Magic, Magician', 224: 'That the Hebrews engaged in magic practices is amply attested in the OT. The repeated prohibition of the use of magic by law, as well as the zealous and fervent struggle waged against it by the prophets, proves how deep-rooted was the belief in the efficacy of this art'.
34 See e.g. Bolt, *Jesus' Defeat of Death*, 33–34; Alexander, 'Incantations and Books of Magic'; Bohak, *Ancient Jewish Magic*. A major cause of persecution of the Jews in medieval times was because of their reputation as 'the magician par excellence', see Trachtenberg, *Jewish Magic*, ch.1.
35 'According to this use, first attested in the LXX in 2 Esr. and 1 Ch., γραμματεύς is a translation of the Heb. סוֹפֵר (Aram. סָפְרָא) which means a "man learned in the Torah," a "rabbi," an "ordained theologian"'; Jeremias, 'γραμματεύς', 1.740.
36 'The high reputation of the rabbis among the people (Mk. 12:38 f.; Mt. 23:6 f.) rested on their knowledge of the Law and oral tradition, and also of secret theosophic, cosmogonic and eschatological doctrines concealed by an esoteric discipline', Jeremias 'γραμματεύς', 1.741. 'The man who claims to be a sage must "know how to answer if he is asked a learned question in any field" *b.Qid.* 49b'; Wilckens, 'σοφία, σοφός', 514–515. n.25.
37 E.g. Ancients: Arnobius, *Adv.Nat.* 1.44; Moderns: Yamauchi, 'Magic, Sorcery', 383, 384.
38 Cross-culturally, one of chief sources of opposition to magic was the established religion; Pharr, 'Interdiction', 278.

was a much-feared βιαιοθάνατος and ἀκέφαλος. Whether or not there may be good outcomes, to operate by such *daemones* was a sign of malevolent magic, almost by definition.[39]

2.3 A Certain *Death-Deserving* Wisdom

With an eye on both OT and Roman law, the Pharisees and Herodians would also agree upon the consequences attached to Jesus' crime. Although beneficent magic was tolerated by most ancient societies, 'the antisocial use of magic was universally condemned and it was legally proscribed in the various ancient peoples—Egyptians, Babylonians, Hebrews, Greeks, and Romans'.[40] The Jewish scriptures associated magic with many other antisocial practices,[41] and, even if it was never stamped out completely, the law was clear that its practitioners were to be put to death (Exod 22:18; Lev 20:6,27)—even if they were close family members (Deut 13:6–10).[42] Like other ancient societies, antisocial or maleficent magic was proscribed by Roman law codes, from the Twelve Tables (ca 450 B.C.) through to Justinian, and placed under the death penalty to be delivered in a variety of horrific forms—including, at least for the slave, crucifixion.[43]

The announcement of the official suspicion that Jesus was a magician and necromancer would have been a happy co-incidence for the Pharisees and Herodians, already seeking a charge against him that might attract a death penalty—even happier, if Antipas's own evidence could be used to persuade the Roman prefect in the right direction (cf. Mark 6:14–16).[44] As it turned out, however, and according to Luke, Antipas—and perhaps the charges of magic with him—crumbled at the last minute (Luke 23:8–15), leaving Jesus to be crucified instead under Pilate's mocking title 'King of the Jews' (Luke 23:38).

Sulla's six-part *Lex Cornelia de sicariis et veneficiis*, especially in its fifth section, was the law that underlay the Roman proscription of magic.[45] The six parts were probably (parts 2–4 are not extant) held together by the notion of 'wrongful death brought about through stealth and malice

---

39 As prescribed for the Jewish context by Deut 18:14–20, and illustrated most aptly by Isaiah 8:19–22. Certainly this was codified in the later Roman legislation, see Theodotion Code 3, 4, 7; Pharr, 'Interdiction', 282, 283, 284.
40 Pharr, 'Interdiction', 209.
41 Mendelsohn, 'Magic, Magician', 225, lists associations with: human sacrifices (Deut 18:10–11; 2 Kings 17:17; 2 Chron 33:6); lies and deceit (Isa 44:25; Jer 27:9–10; Ezek 22:28; Zech 10:2); the adulterer and harlot (Isa 57:3); the oppressor of widow and orphan (Mal 3:5); see also Acts 13:10; Gal 5:19:21; 2 Tim 3:8; Rev 9:21; 18:23; 21:8; 22:15.
42 Jeremias, *Central Message*, 40–41: 'One thing seems certain to me: the events during Jesus' ministry must have forced him to reckon more and more with the inevitability of his own persecution, and even a violent death. He had been reproached with transgression of the Sabbath, with blasphemy and with magic (Mark 3:22b). In each case the crime entailed the punishment of death by stoning with subsequent hanging of the dead body', cf. *m.Sanh.* 7.4 and 6.4 (R. Eliezer).
43 For a convenient collection of the proscriptions in the extant law codes, see Pharr, 'Interdiction', 277–293: of Bacchanalian rites (187 B.C.); the legislation of Sulla, 'the basis of much of the imperial legislation against magic' (81 B.C.); and the later codes of Theodosius (A.D. 438), Justinian (A.D. 533, 534); for the death penalty, see e.g. pp.278, 280, 284, 289. Rives, 'Magic in the XII Tables', argues that the laws originally proscribed practices that were 'later redefined as magical acts', thus becoming precedents for the laws of the later empire (p.290). Rives, 'Magic in Roman Law', considers the Roman proscriptions from the vantage points of Sulla's *Lex Cornelia de sicariis et veneficiis*, Apuleius' trial (ca. 158/9 C.E.) in his *Apology*, and *The Opinions of Paulus* (300 C.E.), and argues for a gradual shift from 'magic' to 'religious deviance'.
44 In dealing with Apuleius' defence that he was not a magician but a philosopher, Rives, 'Magic in Roman Law', 327, notes that the proconsul Claudius Maximus, presiding over the trial, was therefore forced to decide what description was true, each with very different outcomes for the defendant. Since despite previous antipathy Pilate was willing to listen to Antipas, with evidence from this prominent supporter of Rome in support the charge of magic may have had more traction with the Prefect having to make a similar decision in Jesus' case.
45 Pharr, 'Interdict', 279; and the discussions of Rives, 'Magic in the XII Tables Revisited'; 'Magic and Roman Law'.

aforethought'.[46] As one of the many ironies surrounding Jesus' crucifixion, the sixth part of the same law proscribed causing someone to be wrongfully condemned on a capital charge. To find Jesus innocent of any crime (Mark 15:14a; Luke 23:4,14–15,20,22), and yet to have him crucified, made the actions of Pilate and the Jewish leaders an abuse of power tantamount to the sorcery of which he had been accused. But for the first Christians, another power was at work behind the scenes, that of the Lord and his Messiah (Acts 4:25–30; cf. Psalm 2).

3. A Certain Wisdom: Misunderstood in Nazareth

To return to Mark's account, those in the Nazareth synagogue questioned Jesus' word and deed. For sure, he was attracting a crowd with 'these things', that is, with 'a certain wisdom' and miracles 'such as these', but from whence did 'these things' come? The scribes from Jerusalem had already arrived at their answer (3:22–30), and if he was indeed a sorcerer and necromancer, the law was clear. Even if he was a close family member (Deut 13:6–10), he must be handed over. With the Pharisees and Herodians already seeking to kill him (3:6), and despite his family's desire to protect him from the madness with which he was being charged (3:20–21),[47] the people in his hometown established some distance between themselves and their well-known son. Of course he couldn't be the Messiah, he was simply too well known. But the only uncomfortable alternative left them no choice but to reject him.[48]

Mark, however, has been telling a different story. The Spirit of God had come upon Jesus at the Jordan (1:11), and failure to recognise that this was the source of Jesus' activity placed a person in danger of blaspheming the Spirit and missing out on the forgiveness of sins Jesus came to dispense (3:28–29). The Spirit of God had endowed him with the wisdom and power of the promised Messiah (Isa 11:2), and set him on a path towards doing the will of God as the promised Servant of the Lord (Isa 42:1–4), whose strange and mysterious death will come about through human wickedness, but nevertheless end in his triumph (Isa 52:13–53:12). As the Spirit-endowed Servant of the Lord, his ransoming death (10:45) bringing the forgiveness of sins was the last event in God's eschatological timetable before the arrival of the resurrection of the dead and the kingdom of God (9:11–13).[49]

When Mark's readers come to Jesus' rejection in Nazareth for having 'a certain wisdom' (6:2b), but not from God, having been educated by the narrative so far, they are already well on the way to concluding that exactly the opposite is true.

---

46 Rives, 'Magic and Roman Law', 318–319.
47 In 3:21, the subject of ἔλεγον should be taken as a generalising 'they', referring not to Jesus' relatives, but to others. Hearing that others were saying he was mad, Jesus' family acts to protect him from himself by bringing him home.
48 Perhaps unwittingly feeling the force of the actual grammar and syntax (as explained above), some commentators have made the suggestion that the Nazarene's question implied that the source was Satan, without tying it to the specific language in which the question is put; see e.g. Cranfield, *Mark*, 193; Guelich, *Mark*, 309; Collins, *Mark*, 290.
49 See Bolt, *Cross*, 63–64,71–75; 'Forgiveness in Mark's Gospel'.

Bibliography

Alexander, P.S. — 'Incantations and Books of Magic', in E. Schürer et al. (eds.), *The History of the Jewish People in the Age of Jesus Christ*, vol. 3.1 (Edinburgh: T&T Clark, 1986), nos. 32.7, 342–379.

Aune, D. — 'Magic in Early Christianity', in W. Haase (ed.), *ANRW* II.23.2 (Berlin: De Gruyter, 1980), 1507–57.

Bauckham, R. — *Jude and the Relatives of Jesus in the Early Church* (London: T&T Clark [Continuum], 2004 [original: 1990]).

Black, M. — 'Scribe', *IDB* 4.246–248.

Blass, F., A. Debrunner, R.W. Funk — *A Greek Grammar of the New Testament and other Early Christian Literature* (Chicago: University of Chicago Press, 1961). [=BDF]

Blondell, R. — *The Play of Character in Plato's Dialogues* (Cambridge: Cambridge University Press, 2002).

Bohak, G. — *Ancient Jewish Magic: A History* (Cambridge, UK: Cambridge University Press, 2008).

Bolt, P.G. — *The Cross from a Distance. Atonement in Mark's Gospel* (NSBT 18; Downers Grove: InterVarsity Press [Apollos], 2004).

Bolt, P.G. — *Jesus' Defeat of Death. Persuading Mark's Early Readers* (SNTSMS 125; Cambridge: Cambridge University Press, 2003).

Bolt, P.G. — '"With a View to the Forgiveness of Sins": Jesus and Forgiveness in Mark's Gospel', *Reformed Theological Review* 57.2 (1998), 53–69.

Brooks, J.A., & C.L. Winbery — *Syntax of New Testament Greek* (Lanham, MD: University Press of America, 1979).

Charlesworth, J.H. — 'Solomon and Jesus: The Son of David in Ante-Markan Traditions (Mk 10:47)', in L.B. Elder, D.L. Barr, & E.S. Malbon (eds.), *Biblical and Humane: A Festschrift for John F. Priest* (Scholars Press Homage Series 20; Atlanta: Scholars Press, 1996), 125–151.

Collins, A.Y. — *Mark: A Commentary* (Minneapolis: Fortress Press, 2007).

Cranfield, C.E.B. — *The Gospel according to St Mark* (Cambridge: Cambridge University Press, 1959).

Duling, D.C. — 'Solomon, Exorcism, and the Son of David', *HTR* 68 (1975), 235–252.

Evans, C.A. — 'Jesus and Psalm 91 in Light of the Exorcism Scrolls', P.W. Flint, J. Duhaime, & K.S. Baek (eds.), *Celebrating the Dead Sea Scrolls: A Canadian Contribution* (Early Judaism and its Literature 30; Atlanta: Society of Biblical Literature, 2011), 541–555.

Foerster, W. — 'Βεεζεβούλ', *TDNT* 1.605–606.

Fohrer, G., & U. Wilckens,	'σοφία, σοφός', *TDNT* 7.465–528. (Fohrer: 465–496; Wilckens: 496–528).
Goodwin, W.W.	*A Greek Grammar* (London: Macmillan, ²1894, repr. 1987 [1879]).
Guelich, R.A.	*Mark 1–8:26* (WBC 34A; Dallas: Word, 1989).
Harrison, J.R.	*Paul and the Ancient Celebrity Circuit. The Cross and Moral Transformation* (WUNT 430; Tübingen, 2019).
Instone-Brewer, D.	'Jesus of Nazareth's Trial in the Uncensored Talmud', *TynB* 62.2 (2011), 269–294.
Jeremias, J.	'γραμματεύς', *TDNT* 1.740–742.
Jeremias, J.	*The Central Message of the New Testament* (London: SCM, 1965).
Kautzsch, E., & A.E. Cowley	*Gesenius' Hebrew Grammar* (Oxford: Clarendon, 21910, repr. 1983 [German: 281909]).
Korsvoll, N.H.	'Jesus of Nazareth Revisited: Markham J. Geller's Apotropaic Jesus Forty Years Later', *JJMS* 6 (2019), 88–109.
Kraeling, C.H.	'Was Jesus Accused of Necromancy?', *JBL* 59 (1940), 147–57.
McCasland, S.V.	'Magi', *IDB* 3.220–223.
McCown, C.C.	'The Christian Tradition as to the Magical Wisdom of Solomon', *JPOS* 2 (1922), 1–24.
Mendelsohn, I.	'Magic, Magician', *IDB* 3.223–225
Metzger, B.M.	*A Textual Commentary on the Greek New Testament* (New York: United Bible Societies, 21994).
Moule, C.F.D.	*An Idiom Book of New Testament Greek* (Cambridge: Cambridge University Press, 21959, repr. 1982 [1953]).
Pharr, C.	'The Interdiction of Magic in Roman Law', *Transactions and Proceedings of the American Philological Association* 63 (1932), 269–295.
Pixner, B.	*Paths of the Messiah and Sites of the Early Church from Galilee to Jerusalem* (R. Riesner, ed.; K. Meyrick, S. & M. Randall, transls.; San Francisco: Ignatius Press, 2010 [German: 1991]).
Rives, J.B.	'Magic in Roman Law: The Reconstruction of a Crime', *Classical Antiquity* 22.2 (2003), 313–339.
Rives, J.B.	'Magic in the XII Tables Revisited', *Classical Quarterly* 52.1 (2002), 270–290.
Samain, P.	'L'accusation de magie contre le Christ dans les Évangiles', *ETL* 15 (1938), 449–490.
Schaeder, H.H.	'Ναζαρηνός, Ναζωραῖος', *TDNT* 4.874–879.

Smith, M.	*Jesus the Magician* (London: Victor Gollancz, 1978).
Stanton, G.N.	'Jesus of Nazareth: A Magician and a False Prophet Who Deceived God's People?', in J.B. Green & M. Turner (eds.), *Jesus of Nazareth, Lord and Christ: Essays on the Historical Jesus and New Testament Christology* (Grand Rapids: Eerdmans, 1994), 164–180.
Trachtenberg, J.	*Jewish Magic and Superstition: A Study in Folk Religion* (Philadelphia: University of Pennsylvania Press, 2004).
Wallace, D.B.	*Greek Grammar Beyond the Basics* (Grand Rapids: Zondervan, 1996).
Welch, J.W.	'Law, Magic, Miracles and the Trial of Jesus', in J.H. Charlesworth (ed.), *Jesus and Archaeology* (Grand Rapids: Eerdmans, 2006), 349–383.
Yamauchi, E.	'Magic, Sorcery', in C.A. Evans (ed.), *Encyclopedia of the Historical Jesus* (New York & London: Routledge, 2008), 383–384.

Jesus and Asclepius in the Gospel of John

CRAIG A. EVANS

Abstract

In John's Gospel, Jesus' 'signs' authenticate his divine identity and his saving mission. This logic was also found in the Greco-Roman healing cults, especially the cult of Asclepius. Early Christian writers of the second and third centuries appealed to the miracles as proof of Jesus' message and his divine identity, often in contradistinction to the testimonies of healing associated with Asclepius. This essay examines several of these testimonies in order to explore whether the account of the healings of John 5 and 9 were either written in response to Asclepian testimonies, or influenced by them. The Fourth Gospel appears to have made an attempt to commend the greater advantages of Jesus when compared to the Olympian gods, especially Asclepius.

Key Words: John 5; John 9; Asclepius; Epidaurus; miracles of Jesus; healing; apologetics.

The fourth evangelist drives home the point that the miraculous works of Jesus, formally and thematically called 'signs' (σημεῖα) in his Gospel,[1] authenticate the divine identity of Jesus and his saving mission. When challenged for performing a healing on the Sabbath, Jesus tells his critics that 'the works which the Father has granted me to accomplish, these very works which I am doing, bear me witness that the Father has sent me' (John 5:36). Jesus, of course, means he has been sent *from heaven* (cf. John 3:13,31; 6:41–42,50; 7:29)[2] and the miraculous works are proof of this claim. So impressed by his signs, including, above all, the feeding of the five thousand in the wilderness (John 6:1–14), the crowd, many of whom now believe in Jesus, ask, 'When the Christ appears, will he do more signs [πλείονα σημεῖα ποιήσει] than this man has done?' (John 7:31). Both context and grammar imply that the answer is, 'No, indeed not'.[3]

When asked if he is the Messiah, Jesus replies, 'I told you, and you do not believe. The works

---

1   The σημεῖα are part of Jesus's 'work' (ἔργον) or 'works' (ἔργα), which he must 'do' (ποιεῖν) or 'work' (ἐργάζεσθαι). See John 4:34; 5:17, 19, 30, 36; 6:30; 7:3; 10:32.
2   Prophets are 'sent' (שׁלח / ἀποστέλλειν) by God to speak to people (e.g. Isa 6:8; 61:1; Jer 1:7; 7:25; 14:14–15; 19:14; 25:4; 26:5, 12, 15; 29:19; 35:15; 44:4; Ezek 2:3–4; 3:5–6; Obad 1; Hag 1:12; Zech 2:8–9, 11; 4:9; 6:15; 7:12; Mal 3:1; 4:5), and are in fact called 'sent ones' or 'apostles' (שליחים), but they are not sent *from heaven*. In the fourth Gospel Jesus is *sent* (usually ἀποστέλλειν, though sometimes πέμπειν)—and this is said frequently—and on one occasion he is himself called an ἀπόστολος, 'one sent' (cf. John 13:16). For relevant lexical data, see Rengstorf, 'ἀποστέλλω'.
3   ὁ χριστὸς ὅταν ἔλθῃ μὴ πλείονα σημεῖα ποιήσει ὧν οὗτος ἐποίησεν; could be translated, 'When the Messiah should come, he will not do more signs than this one has done, will he?' The question is almost rhetorical and clearly expects a negative response.

that I do in my Father's name, they bear witness to me [τὰ ἔργα ἃ ἐγὼ ποιῶ ἐν τῷ ὀνόματι τοῦ πατρός μου ταῦτα μαρτυρεῖ περὶ ἐμοῦ]' (John 10:25). As it turns out, the works that Jesus does in his Father's name justify his startling claim, 'I and the Father are one' (John 10:31). Rightly sensing the potentially blasphemous nature of such a claim, Jesus' critics threaten to stone him (John 10:31 ἐβάστασαν πάλιν λίθους οἱ Ἰουδαῖοι ἵνα λιθάσωσιν αὐτόν; cf. 8:59). This threat and the context in which it is uttered unmistakably allude to Deuteronomy 13, where Moses warns Israel against a false prophet who tries to lead the people into idolatry and the worship of false gods. Anyone who attempts to do this is to be stoned (cf. LXX Deut 13:11 'they shall stone him with stones [λιθοβολήσουσιν αὐτὸν ἐν λίθοις], and he shall die because he sought to turn you away from the Lord your God'). Jesus has not transgressed a contentious point of Pharisaic halakah; he has violated—or so it seems—a foundational prohibition in Torah.

To rebut the charge of blasphemy, Jesus once again appeals to his works: 'If I am not doing the works of my Father, then do not believe me; but if I do them, even though you do not believe me, believe the works [τοῖς ἔργοις πιστεύετε], that you may know and understand that the Father is in me and I am in the Father' (John 10:37–38). That is, if Jesus really is doing the works of his Father, then he commits no blasphemy, nor has he violated Torah, in claiming that he and the Father are one.

Appeal to the 'works' (ἔργα) that are being done reflects the logic of knowing the quality of something by its 'fruit' (Matt 12:33; Luke 6:43–44). It is in that sense that Jesus exhorts skeptics to 'believe the works'. In effect, he reasons that if the skeptics are unable to believe *in him*, they at least should be able to believe *in the works* that he is doing. In Johannine language the works that Jesus performs are 'signs' (σημεῖα), which mostly reflect Mosaic tradition (esp. John 6:14), as expressed both in Scripture and in subsequent interpretation, and shed light on the identity and mission of Jesus.

But the logic expressed here is not limited to the world of Jewish Scripture and tradition. It is very much found in the world of the Greco-Roman healing cults, with which the present study is concerned. With respect to the cult of Asclepius countless inscribed testimonials are extant that describe healings. The apologetic purpose of the Asclepian testimonials is well recognized and a few of them will be discussed below.

After Jesus raises Lazarus (John 11:38–44), many people, 'who had come with Mary and had seen what he did, believed in him' (John 11:45)—we have here an example of people believing in Jesus because they 'believed the works'. In reaction to the raising of Lazarus, the religious leaders ask themselves, 'What are we to do? For this man performs many signs [πολλὰ ποιεῖ σημεῖα]' (John 11:47). During Passion Week Jesus exhorts his disciples, 'Believe me that I am in the Father and the Father in me; or else believe me for the sake of the works themselves' (John 14:11). The logic here is the same as expressed earlier in John 10:37–38. Both friend and foe alike are to recognize that the works that Jesus performs demonstrate his close connection with God and that therefore with justification he may say he comes from heaven and is one with the Father.

Finally, at the conclusion of the Gospel, where the author gives explicit expression to his purpose for writing, we are told: 'Now Jesus did many other signs [πολλὰ μὲν οὖν καὶ ἄλλα σημεῖα ἐποίησεν ὁ Ἰησοῦς] in the presence of the disciples, which are not written in this book; but these are written that you may believe that the Christ, the Son of God, is Jesus and that believing you may have life in his name' (John 20:30–31).[4] There can be little doubt that the signs/works performed

---

4 On how John 20:31 should be rendered, see Carson, *John*, 662. The subject is 'the Christ, the Son of God' (ὁ χριστὸς ὁ υἱὸς τοῦ θεοῦ). The anarthrous Ἰησοῦς ('Jesus'), which occurs near the beginning of the clause, is not the subject but the predicate.

by Jesus serve an important theological and apologetic purpose in the fourth Gospel. These signs/works demonstrate that Jesus is indeed the Son of God and giver of life.[5]

The Apologetic Value of the Miracles of Jesus

The apologetic of the fourth Gospel is well developed, to be sure, and is very much focused on the theme of the fulfillment of Scripture, especially those texts invoked in reference to aspects of Jesus' rejection, suffering, and death.[6] But closely linked to this scriptural apologetic are the miracles, or signs. The signs are the works that demonstrate that Jesus has indeed come from heaven. This apologetic, however, did not originate with the fourth evangelist, for the apologetic value of the miracles of Jesus was probably recognized as early as the *Sitz im Leben Jesu*. But this apologetic was not limited to the time of Jesus and his apostles. The miracles had great apologetic value in the second and third centuries, playing an important role in Christian expansion in the Roman Empire.

Early Christian writers often appealed to the miracles as proof not only of the truth of Jesus's message but of his divine identity. The earliest testimony of this nature is credited to the apologist Quadratus (died ca 140). According to Eusebius, the apologist claimed:

> The works of our Savior were always present, for they were true, those that were healed, those that were raised from the dead, who were seen not only when they were healed and when they were raised, but were also constantly present, not only while the Savior was on earth, but also after his departure, they remained for quite a while, so that some of them survived even to our day.[7] (*apud* Eusebius, *Historia ecclesiastica* 4.3.2)

In his reply to Trypho's expressions of skepticism, Justin Martyr (*c.* 100 – *c.* 165) claims that the miracles performed by Jesus 'compelled those who lived at that time to recognise him':

> Christ ... appeared among your people, and healed those who were maimed, and deaf, and lame in body from their birth, causing them to leap, to hear, and to see, by his word. And having raised the dead, and making them to live, and by his works he compelled those who lived at that time to recognise him.[8] (*Dialogos cum Tryphone* 69.7)

The healings and rescucitations, says Justin, 'compelled' (ἐδυσώπει) Jesus's contemporaries to 'recognise him' (ἐπιγνῶναι αὐτόν), that is, to recognise his divine identity (which is reminiscent of John's use of γινώσκειν).[9] Justin's choice of the verb δυσωπεῖν, which does not occur in New Testament writings and not often elsewhere in early Christian literature, calls for comment, for

---

5 Rightly Smith, *Johannine Christianity*, 176–77: the signs of Jesus in the fourth Gospel raise 'the question of Jesus' identity'. These signs, or works, hint at Jesus's divinity, a feature that later Christian writers will exploit. On this point, see Ensor, *Jesus and His 'Works'*. That the signs of the fourth Gospel point to the divinity of Jesus seems a bit more obvious, in my opinion, than Ensor allows. He is correct, however, in his observations of their exploitation by later Fathers of the Church.
6 See Bittner, *Jesu Zeichen im Johannesevangelium*; Obermann, *Die christologische Erfüllung*; Berger, *Im Anfang war Johannes*, 166–70. Although this is not the place to pursue the question at length, it is interesting to note that Berger (169–70) suggests that the function of miracles in the fourth Gospel is closer to that of the Synoptics than is usually recognized and that the fourth Gospel therefore should be assigned an earlier date.
7 Translation based on Lake, *Eusebius Ecclesiastical History I*, 309.
8 Translation based on Roberts & Donaldson, *The Ante-Nicene Fathers*, 1:233.
9 John 6:49 ('we have believed, and have come to know, that you are the Holy One of God'); 8:28 ('then you will know that I am he'); 10:38 ('that you may know and understand that the Father is in me').

it often means to 'embarrass' or 'persuade by producing shame' (cf. LSJ).[10] By using it, Justin seems to be implying that Jesus's miracles, which the Jewish leadership tried to discredit, put this contrary leadership to shame, leaving it with no excuse for having rejected Jesus.

A generation later Irenaeus (c. 130 – c. 200) speaks about the healing taking place 'in the name of Jesus Christ':

> Others still, heal the sick by laying their hands upon them, and they are made whole. Yes, moreover, as I have said, the dead even have been raised up, and remained among us for many years. And what more shall I say? It is not possible to name the number of the gifts which the Church, (scattered) throughout the whole world, has received from God, in the name of Jesus Christ.[11] (Irenaeus, *Adversus haereses* 2.32.4)

In a number of passages Origen (c. 185 – c. 254) appeals to the healings and exorcisms that take place in the name of Jesus. Indeed, says Origen,

> We affirm that the whole human world has evidence of the work of Jesus since in it dwell the churches of God, which consist of people converted through Jesus from countless evils. Moreover, the name of Jesus [τὸ ὄνομα τοῦ Ἰησου] still takes away distractions of mind [ἐκστάσεις ... διανοίας] from men, and demons and diseases [δαίμονας ... καὶ νόσους] as well, and implants a wonderful meekness and tranquility of character, and a love of humanity and a kindness and gentleness, in those who have not feigned to be Christians on account of their need of the necessities of life or some other want, but have genuinely accepted the gospel about God and Christ and the judgment to come.[12] (*Contra Celsum* 1.67)

Celsus clearly understood that at the heart of Christian apologetic was defence of the divinity of Jesus; and the miracles offered powerful evidence in support of this apologetic: 'Celsus ... says, "We deem Jesus to be the Son of God, because he healed the lame and the blind" [ἐνομίσαμεν αὐτὸν εἶναι υἱὸν θεοῦ, ἐπεὶ χωλοὺς καὶ τυφλοὺς ἐθεράπευσε]. ... That he raised the dead ... is not something made up [νεκροὺς ἀνίστη ... οὐκ ἔστι πλάσμα]' (2.48). What Celsus is alleged to have asserted is quite correct; early Christians did in fact 'deem him (Jesus) to be the Son of God, because he healed the lame and the blind'. Of course, Celsus himself believed Jesus performed miracles—but not because he was divine, but because he had learned sorcery in Egypt! (1.28; cf. 2.9, 48, where Origen refers to the charge that Jesus was in league with Satan; Matt 12:24).

Not only do the miracles in the name of Jesus continue to bring people to faith in Origen's time, they did so in the time of Jesus: 'We must observe also that the stupendous acts of (Christ's) power [αἱ τεράστιοι δυνάμεις] were able to bring to faith those of Christ's own time' (*Commentarii in evangelium Joannis* 2.34[28]). The miracles point to the divinity of Jesus, or, in Christian confessional parlance, to his identity as 'Son of God', a confession that lies at the heart of conversion to the Christian faith. The miracles of Jesus—past and present—continue to elicit faith.

What is also noticeable in Patristic apologetical appeal to the miracles of Jesus are attacks leveled against the healing miracles that are associated with the cult of Asclepius. For example,

---

10 δυσωπεῖν means 'to produce a disagreeable expression on the countenance ... [to] persuade by exciting a sense of shame'; cf. Donnegan, *A New Greek and English Lexicon*, 480. Epictetus remarks: 'I have not been shamed [οὐκ ἐδυσωπήθην] by such a person' (*Diatribai* 4.18); and Irenaeus says, '[O]thers of them are ashamed [αἱ δὲ δυσωπούμεναι]' to confess (*Adversus haereses* 1.13.7). There are several good examples in Philo (*De opificio mundi* 128; *Quod deterius potiori insidari soleat* 146; *De posteritate Caini* 97; et al.).
11 Translation based on Roberts & Donaldson, *The Ante-Nicene Fathers*, 1:409.
12 Translation based on Chadwick, *Origen: Contra Celsum*, 62.

Justin Martyr complains that 'when we say we say he made well the lame and paralytics and those blind from birth and that he raised the dead, our saying these things will seem to be like the things said to have been done by Asclepius' (*1 Apologia* 22.6); and anytime the pagans learn of the healings performed by Jesus 'they introduced Asclepius' (54.10). Justin adds to his apologetic by claiming that stories told about Asclepius are plagiarized from the Old Testament prophecies that speak of Christ. Indeed, it isn't only the pagans who put forward Asclepius as a rival of the true Savior; it is the Devil himself, as Justin explains to Trypho: 'And when he (the devil) brings forward Asclepius as the raiser of the dead and healer of all diseases, may I not say that in this matter likewise he has imitated the prophecies about Christ [τὰς περὶ Χριστοῦ ὁμοίως προφητείας μεμιμῆσθαι]?'[13] (*Dialogos cum Tryphone* 69.4). Tertullian ramps up the rhetoric when he calls Asclepius a 'dangerous beast' (*periculosam bestiam*) who supposedly escaped to heaven, to whom pagans now foolishly offer sacrifice (*Ad nationes* 2.14). Other Fathers take swipes at the cult of Asclepius (e.g., Theophilus, *Ad Autolycum* 1.13; 3.2; Origen, *Contra Celsum* 3.22–25; 5.2; Lactantius, *Divinae institutiones* 4.27.12; Arnobius, *Adversus nationes* 1.48.1–2).

So why were the early Fathers so defensive with respect to the healing cult of Asclepius? I think it is because they rightly recognized that the long-established, time-honored cult of Asclepius represented serious competition for the early Christian movement. From a pagan point of view, the principal benefit that the Christ of the Christians offered was healing. If Christ could heal, then perhaps the other things that Christians say about him are true. But if Christ were no better at healing than was Asclepius and his therapeutic priests, then why follow Christ and incur the risks and disadvantages that are part of belonging to a movement that is illegal in the eyes of the state and is sometimes violently persecuted?

The Healing Cult of Asclepius

The earliest known reference to Asclepius is found in Homer, where he is depicted as a mortal physician (*Ilias* 2.731–732; 4.193–194: 'summon Machaon, son of Asclepius, the noble physician [ἀμύμονος ἰητῆρος]'). We think that it was in the sixth century BCE that Asclepius was deified and said to be the son of Apollo. In the centuries that followed his myth grew and his popularity increased. In the first three centuries of the Christian Church, worship of Asclepius, the healing god, took place everywhere in the Roman Empire.[14] The competition between the healers Christ and Asclepius was part of a larger competition centered on miracles.[15]

We shall review a few examples of the healing testimonies and compare them to healing stories in the Gospel of John. The purpose of this comparative study is to explore the possibility that the story of the healing of the infirm man at the pool in John 5 is either in response to the cult of Asclepius or has been influenced by the cult. We raise the same question with respect to the healing of the man born blind in John 9. The four Asclepian testimonies below are from inscriptions at Epidaurus. They relate the stories of a blind man who regained his sight and three men described variously as paralyzed or lame.

---

13 Translations are based on Minns & Parvis, *Justin*, 137, 139, 225; and Roberts & Donaldson, *The Ante-Nicene Fathers*, 1:233.
14 As Ludwig Edelstein puts it in Edelstein & Edelstein, *Asclepius*, 2:108: '[W]orship (of Asclepius) spread everywhere; it became one of the most renowned among the many ancient cults; it outlasted most of them; it was the hated enemy and dreaded competitor of Christianity'. For a recent and succinct description of the cult of Asclepius and his daughter Hygieia, see Charlesworth, *Good and Evil Serpent*, 160–167, 529–32 (notes).
15 Remus, *Pagan-Christian Conflict*.

The testimony of Valerius Aper:

> To Valerius Aper, a blind soldier [στρατιώτῃ τυφλῷ], the god [ὁ θεός] revealed that he should go and take the blood of a white cock along with honey and compound an eye salve and for three days should apply [ἐπιχρεῖσαι] it to his eyes. And he could see again [ἀνέβλεψεν] and went and publicly offered thanks to the god [τῷ θεῷ].[16] (IG XIV.966 [=SIG III.1173], lines 12–15)

There are many references in literature to those healed of blindness thanks to Asclepius. Aristides (129–189 C.E.), who used to sing the praises of Asclepius at every opportunity, speaks of a special water, which takes the place of a drug. 'When bathed with it many recovered their eyesight' (*Oratio* 29.15).

The testimony of Hermodicos of Lampsacus:

> Hermodicos of Lampsacus, paralyzed of body [ἀκρατὴς τοῦ σώματος]. When he was sleeping here, he was healed [ἰάσατο] and was ordered, when he went out, to carry into the sanctuary the biggest stone that he could. He brought the one that lies in front of the Abaton.[17] (Epidaurus stele A lines 107–110 [=IG IV² 1.121–122])

Figure 1. Statue of Asclepius, with staff and snake, recovered from Epidauros, where a major Asclepian centre thrived for centuries. Photo courtesy of Lee Martin McDonald.

The testimony of Nicanor:

> Nicanor, lame [χωλός]. When he was sitting down, being awake, some boy grabbed his crutch and ran away. Getting up he ran after him and from this he became well [ὑγιὴς ἐγένετο].[18] (Epidaurus stele A lines 111–112 [=IG IV2 1.121–122])

---

16 Text and translation based on Edelstein & Edelstein, *Asclepius*, 1:251.
17 Text and translation based on LiDonnici, *Epidaurian Miracle Inscriptions*, 96–97; cf. Edelstein & Edelstein, *Asclepius*, 1:222, 232.
18 Text and translation based on LiDonnici, *Epidaurian Miracle Inscriptions*, 96–97; cf. Edelstein & Edelstein, *Asclepius*, 1:224, 233.

The testimony of a lame man of Epidaurus:

> ... from Epidaurus, lame [χωλός]. This man [came to the sanctuary carried on a litter.] Sleeping here, he saw a vision. [It seemed to him the god ...] and ordered him [to bring out] a ladder [and climb] up on the sanctuary. He ... fell and up on ... a little [down] the ladder. Asclepius at first was angry at these things ... though lame, when da[y came ... well he] left [ἐξῆλθε].[19] (Epidaurus stele B lines 86–95)

In most of the testimonials those healed slept in the sanctuary, in one of the porticoes. While sleeping the god Asclepius comes to the suppliants in a dream, either healing them with a surgical procedure or with a drug, or providing instructions that upon waking, if followed, will result in healing. In the case of Valerius Aper a salve is to be prepared and applied to the eyes. In the case of Hermodicos he is ordered to pick up a heavy stone and bring it to the sanctuary. This action both completes and demonstrates the reality of the healing. In the case of Nicanor it is in his pursuit of the boy who snatched his crutch that he regained his ability to walk and run. The pursuit, of course, provided evidence of the cure. And in the case of the unnamed man of Epidaurus, he is directed to undertake a task (the exact nature of which is not clear because of the lacunose condition of the inscription), which resulted in healing. At one point Asclepius is said to be angry, perhaps because of a lack of faith (and this theme appears in other Asclepian testimonials). In any event, the man departs from the sanctuary whole.

There are many such testimonials at Epidaurus and elsewhere. It is estimated that there may have been as many as four hundred healing temples and sanitariums in the Greco-Roman world dedicated to Asclepius. The best known shrines were located at Athens, Corinth, Cos, Epidaurus, and Pergamum.[20] Other deities, such as Apollo and Isis, offered healing, of course, but the cult of Asclepius was by far the most popular. Part of the attraction was the sympathetic portrait of Asclepius, which stood in contrast to the unfeeling, fickle, and often capricious Olympian deities.[21]

John and the Healing Cult of Asclepius

Two healings in John potentially offer the closest parallels to the healing testimonies found inscribed at Epidaurus. I shall first consider the healing of the blind man in John 9 and then the healing of the disabled man in John 5. The latter story seems to offer the closest parallels with Asclepian tradition.

A man born blind:

> As he [Jesus] passed by, he saw a man blind from his birth. ... he spat on the ground and made clay of the spittle and anointed the man's eyes with the clay [ἔπτυσεν χαμαὶ καὶ ἐποίησεν πηλὸν ἐκ τοῦ πτύσματος καὶ ἐπέχρισεν αὐτοῦ τὸν πηλὸν ἐπὶ τοὺς ὀφθαλμούς], saying

---

19 Text and translation based on LiDonnici, *Epidaurian Miracle Inscriptions*, 110–13; cf. Edelstein & Edelstein, *Asclepius*, 1:227–28, 236.
20 For pertinent bibliography relating to archaeology at these sites, see Avalos, *Health Care*, 50, 129–30.
21 This important point is underscored in Edelstein & Edelstein, *Asclepius*, 2:74, 84, 111–12; Cotter, 'Miracles Stories', esp. 168: 'But the devotion to Asclepius warmed due to his great humanity, his compassionate concern for continued life and health for all devotees no matter what their social stratum, and the absence of any myths of selfishness around him'.

to him, 'Go, wash in the pool of Siloam' (which means Sent).²² So he went and washed and came back seeing. (John 9:1, 6–7, RSV)

I have omitted the dialogue (vv. 2–5), in which the disciples ask Jesus the cause of the man's blindness from birth, as well as the polemical and didactic material that follows (vv. 8–41). We are told that the man Jesus healed was 'blind from his birth' (τυφλὸν ἐκ γενετῆς). According to the *Testament of Solomon*, evil spirits can cause blindness while infants are 'in the wombs of women [ἐν κοιλίαις γυναικῶν]' (T. Sol. 12:2a).²³ The recovery of sight for those born blind was apparently quite rare, perhaps 'unheard of', as the healed man himself says to those who are questioning him (John 9:32). Indeed, there are no examples in Israel's ancient Scripture of the recovery of sight of one born blind.²⁴ From a modern medical perspective, the recovery of sight in the case of one born without eyesight would indeed be unheard of in ancient times. One Asclepian testimony offers an approximate parallel. We are told that a man had no eyeball, that his eyesocket was empty. In his sleep Asclepius prepared a concoction, poured it into the empty socket, and the man awoke in the morning able to see (Epidaurus stele A lines 72–79 [=IG IV² 1.121–122]).

In John 9 Jesus makes use of spittle. (In Mark 8:22–26 Jesus spat into the eyes of a blind man.) In the Johannine story Jesus makes clay and 'anoints' the man's eyes,²⁵ which parallels the testimony of Valerius Aper who was instructed to make and apply a salve on his eyes.²⁶ But in the case of the blind man of John 9 it isn't simply the clay made of spittle and earth, it is the washing in the pool of Siloam that effects the healing. Thanks largely to association with the prophet Isaiah, the pool of Siloam, whose first-century location has only recently been identified,²⁷ had acquired an interesting reputation. The sporadic 'sending' forth of water, which apparently gave the pool its name, was linked to Isaiah and was thought to be providential (cf. *Lives of the Prophets* 1:1–5).²⁸

There is more. According to ben Sira (*c*. 180 BCE), Isaiah the prophet 'was great and faithful in his vision.²³ In his days the sun went backward, and he lengthened the life of the king' (Sir 48:22–23). The venerable sage goes on to praise Isaiah for his prophetic foresight, which included

---

22 The Old Greek transliterates שִׁלֹחַ, *šilōaḥ*, understood to mean 'sent' (from שׁלח), as Siloam (Σιλωάμ). See Isa 8:6. It is not certain, however, that this was the original meaning of the word.
23 The language of the *Testament of Solomon* is closer to Semitic expression than is the language in John. As examples, Samson is to be a Nazarite 'from the womb [ἐκ τῆς γαστρός]' (Jdg 13:5), while Israel is rebuked for being a rebel 'from the belly [ἐκ κοιλίας]' (Isa 48:8). Elsewhere in the New Testament we find this Semitic style of expression. It is seen in Matt 19:12, where one is said to be eunuch 'from the womb of the mother' (ἐκ κοιλίας μητρός), or in Acts 3:2, where the man's lameness was 'from the womb of his mother' (ἐκ κοιλίας μητρὸς αὐτοῦ). It is not obvious, therefore, that *T. Sol.* 12:2a has been influenced by John 9, whose expression, ἐκ γενετῆς ('from birth'), doesn't reflect the typical Semitic pattern. The reference to 'Place of the Skull' (τόπου ἐγκεφάλου) in *T. Sol.* 12:3 is almost certainly a Christian element, though again its language is not a close match with the language in the Gospels: In Matt 27:33 and Mark 15:22 we have κρανίου τόπος, while in Luke 23:33 we have τὸν τόπον τὸν καλούμενον κρανίον.
24 The righteous Tobias regained his sight (Tob 11:12–13), but he had not been born blind.
25 Followers of Asclepius 'smear themselves with clay [μετὰ χειμῶνα]' (Aristides, *Oratio* 48.74).
26 The salve was made with 'honey and the blood of a white cock'. Apparently the blood of a white cock was believed to possess healing powers, for apparently King Pyrrhus customarily sacrificed a white cock to effect healing (cf. Plutarch, *Pyrrhus* 3.4–5). We have an early reference to a cock sacrificed to Asclepius in the dying words of Socrates, 'Crito, we owe a cock to Asclepius. Pay it and do not neglect it' (Plato, *Phaedo* 118A).
27 The pool was discovered in 2004 by archaeologist Eli Shukron. See Reich, Shukron, & Lernau, 'Recent Discoveries', esp. 163–66; Shanks, 'Siloam Pool'; von Wahlde, 'Pool of Siloam'. See also Josephus, *J.W.* 5.140.
28 According to v. 2: 'God did the sign of Siloam because of the prophet, because before he died, being faint, he prayed to drink water and immediately it was sent to him from it. For this reason it was called Siloam, which translated means "sent"'.

knowledge of hidden and future things (48:24–25). But it was Isaiah's involvement in the healing of Hezekiah, to which ben Sira makes reference, that was truly remarkable: Isaiah heals the king's infection with a cake of figs and as proof that the king will live for another fifteen years, the shadow cast by the sun reverses its direction (cf. 2 Kgs 20:6–11; Isa 38:5–8). It seems that ben Sira's summary of the prophet's ministry 'serves to make Isaiah appear to be all the more a miracle-worker'.[29]

One must wonder if in the time of Jesus the pool of Siloam was viewed as in some sense sacred, even potent,[30] whose waters might possess curative powers. Apparently some people believed something like this with respect to the pool of Bethzatha/Bethesda (John 5:2), which will be discussed below. The legendary connection to Isaiah, believed to have miraculous healing power at his disposal, would have added to this reputation. The fourth evangelist may well have known some of this tradition.[31] Moreover, we find in both Jewish sources,[32] as well as Asclepian, traditions that express beliefs that bathing in sacred pools or waters could result in healing. (The Asclepian traditions will be explored below in connection with the pool of Bethzatha/Bethesda story in John 5.).

There is biblical precedent for this thinking in Jewish tradition. Recall Elisha who commanded Naaman the Syrian captain to 'go, wash in the Jordan', in order to be cleansed of his leprosy (2 Kgs 5:10–13), even as Jesus commanded the blind man to 'go, wash' in the pool of Siloam (John 9:7), in order to regain his sight. Initially Naaman is angry because, as he put it to his servant, 'Are not Abana and Pharpar, the rivers of Damascus, better than all the waters of Israel? Could I not wash in them, and be clean?' (2 Kgs 5:12). As it turns out, his healing takes place in the Jordan River, the river Israel crossed when the people entered the land of promise (Josh 4:1–7). After washing in the Jordan, Naaman is restored and confesses, 'I know that there is no God in all the earth but in Israel' (2 Kgs 5:15). Washing in the Jordan not only healed Naaman's body, it impacted him spiritually. Washing in the Pool of Siloam not only restored the blind man's sight, it restored his purity and made entry into the sacred temple precincts possible.[33] It also gave him greater spiritual insight, as becomes clear in the debate with the Pharisees that follows.

Most of the healings of blindness in the Asclepian testimonies are unparalled in early Christian tradition. Here we are thinking of the Epidaurian testimonies that claim the god prepared a φάρμακον of one sort or another and poured it into an empty eye socket or performed surgery on an eye. Nothing like this is reported in the New Testament Gospels. Jesus administers no φάρμακα and he performs no surgeries.

---

29 Lee, *Studies*, 212. Lee goes on to note rightly that ben Sira regular stresses the miraculous element in his summaries of Israel's past heroes.
30 From the pool of Siloam water was drawn for use in libations in the temple precincts during the festival of Tabernacles (*m. Sukkah* 4:9 'They used to fill a golden flagon … with water from Siloam …'). For description of the rabbinic materials and commentary on John 7:37–38, where on the occasion of the Feast of Tabernacles Jesus speaks of the living water he provides, see Jeremias, 'λίθος, λίθινος', 277–78.
31 As is carefully reviewed in Young, 'A Study', esp. 216–21.
32 Shemesh, 'Therapeutic Bathing'.
33 The point is made by von Wahlde, 'Pool of Siloam', 173.

The invalid at the pool of Bethzatha/Bethesda:

> Now there is in Jerusalem by the Sheep Gate a pool, in Hebrew called Bethzatha (or Bethesda),[34] which has five porticoes. In these lay a multitude of sick, blind, lame, withered [τῶν ἀσθενούντων, τυφλῶν, χωλῶν, ξηρῶν[35]]. One man was there, who had been ill for thirty-eight years. When Jesus saw him and knew that he had been lying there a long time, he said to him, 'Do you want to be healed?' The sick man answered him, 'Sir, I have no man to put me into the pool when the water is troubled, and while I am going another steps down before me'. Jesus said to him, 'Rise, take up your pallet, and walk'. And at once the man was healed, and he took up his pallet and walked. (John 5:2–9, RSV, modified)

We are not told precisely what the invalid's problem was. He obviously could not walk but had to be carried (as the references to his pallet and the lack of a man to assist him make clear); so he probably was 'lame' or 'paralyzed' (either χωλός or ξηρός). So why, after thirty-eight years, has the man failed to be healed by the agitated waters of this pool? The idea seems to be that the man has failed because only one person can be healed whenever the pool is agitated and because the sick man has no one to assist him, he is never first into the water. The scribe who added the gloss in v. 4 ('the first one entering after the troubling of the water was made whole')

Figure 2. Excavations at Saint Anne's Church, Jerusalem, the location of the Pool of Bethesda. Photo public domain.

---

34 There is confusion in the manuscript tradition with respect to the name of this pool. The earliest readings (Βηθσαϊδά in 𝔓[75] B W, Βηδσαϊδά in 𝔓[66c]), are probably assimilations to the well known home village of Peter, Andrew, and Philip (cf. John 1:44). Another fairly early reading is Βηθεσδά (C, accepted by the SBLGNT and the TNGNT) and variants Βηθεσεδά (E*) and Βησθεσδά (N), which may have support in the Copper Scroll's בית אשדתין (3Q15 11.12). The NA[28] and UBSGNT[4] accept Βηθζαθά (‭א‬ 33 Eusebius; L: Βηζαθά), though with some hesitation. See the discussion in Metzger, *Textual Commentary*, 208.

35 D (followed by some versions, mostly old Italian) adds παραλυτικῶν, 'paralytics'. This is probably an old scribal gloss. Note, too, that I have omitted the glosses at vv. 3b–4, which in many mss read something like this: ... παραλυτικῶν ἐκδεχομένων τὴν τοῦ ὕδατος κίνησιν. ἄγγελος [κυρίου] γὰρ κατὰ καιρὸν κατέβαινεν ἐν τῇ κολυμβήθρᾳ, καὶ ἐτάρασσε τὸ ὕδωρ· ὁ οὖν πρῶτος ἐμβὰς μετὰ τὴν ταραχὴν τοῦ ὕδατος, ὑγιὴς ἐγίνετο, ᾧ δήποτε κατείχετο νοσήματι, '... paralytics awaiting the movement of the water. For an angel [of the Lord] went down at a certain season into the pool, and troubled the water; then the first one entering after the troubling of the water was made whole of whatever disease he had'. Evidently the angel agitating the water was part of the legend surrounding the pool of Bethzatha/Bethesda. The legend probably gave rise to the glosses, which in turn only added color and credibility to the legend.

evidently understood the tradition this way. Another possibility is that by the time the crippled man manages to get to the water, the agitation has ceased. Others who made it in before him were made well.

It was mentioned above in the discussion concerning the man who regained his sight after washing in the pool of Siloam (John 9) that traditions of special pools and waters with oracular and healing powers were entertained in Greco-Roman and Jewish traditions. Temples were often built by springs (Pausanias, *Graeciae descriptio* 1.14.1; 1.28.4; 1.34.4; 2.5.1; 3.20.7; 3.25.4; 3.26.1; 4.31.1, 6; 4.33.1, 4; 4.36.7; 6.22.7; 7.5.2; 7.21.13; 7.22.4; 7.24.3; 8.13.2; 8.19.2; 8.35.8; and many more). Some of these temples erected adjacent to springs are dedicated to Asclepius (e.g., 1.21.4 [Athens]; 2.2.3 [Cenchreae]; 3.21.2 [Pellana], 8 [Cythium]; 5.11.11 [Epidaurus]).[36] Pausanias tells us that there is in Patrae adjacent a sanctuary of Demeter a spring (πηγή), next to which is an 'infallible oracle' (μαντεῖον … ἀψευδές) in matters relating to those who are sick (*Graeciae descriptio* 7.21.12; cf. 1.34.3). Legend has it, Pausanias learned in his travels, that the goddess Hera bathes every year in a spring near Nauplia to recover her maidenhood (2.38.2). Many other events of great importance could be mentioned—whether historical or mythological—that took place near springs.

Of course, for most people it was the curative powers of certain springs, pools, and wells that were important. Belief in the curative power of water was ancient and widespread. According to a first-century manuscript of the Egyptian Book of Dead (P.Rhind I col. vi), 'you are made clean with the water that comes from the Elephantine' (that is, what was believed to be the headwaters of the Nile River). As part of his induction into the mysteries of Isis, Apuleius, only recently restored to human form, is washed and purified (*Metamorphoses* 11.23 *purissime circumrorans abluit*).[37] Pausanias reports that at the village of Heracleia was one such spring. 'Those who bathe in the spring', he says, 'are cured of all sorts of aches and pains' (6.22.7). In Samicum is a spring in a cave, whose waters cure those whose skin has lost its color thanks to vitiligo (5.5.11). It was the custom, at least in some places, to throw a coin into the sacred spring, 'when a man has been cured of a disease' (1.34.4).

Most healing sanctuaries were adjacent to water of one sort or another. Water was especially important for the cult of Asclepius.[38] No one had more positive things to say about the benefits of pools, springs, and wells associated with Asclepius than Aelius Aristides. Throughout his *Oratio* Aristides sings the praises of the god's sacred water. In a speech in honor of Asclepius stating how the god cures his followers in paradoxical and unexpected ways, we are told that the god prescribes ablutions of cold water, when one expects warm, and stopping colds and influenza by 'baths in rivers' (*Oratio* 42.8), when one expects to keep dry. The god knows best. By bathing in the waters of Asclepius 'many recovered their eyesight' (39.14). Drinking these sacred waters sometimes leads to mantic powers (39.15), which recalls what Pausanias said about the spring near Patrae, whose oracles were said never to fail. 'Purifications', says Aristides, 'took place near the river' (50.6). Devotees, he also says, 'smear themselves with clay in honor of the god' Asclepius (48.74).

In his *Oratio* Aristides offers readers two panegyrics for the Asclepian wells of Epidaurus and Pergamum. With regard to the former (*Oratio* 39.1–18), which is lengthier and more detailed than the latter, Aristides speaks of its 'beauty and taste', of drinking it and bathing in it (39.1).

---

36 More than three hundred sites related to Asclepius have been identified. For a list of these sites, see Walton, *Cult of Asklepios*, 95–121. More sites have been discovered since the appearance of Walton's study. It is now estimated that there may have been as many as four hundred.

37 Both texts are discussed in Reitzenstein, *Die Hellenistischen Mysterienreligionen*, 88–89.

38 Walton, *Cult of Asklepios*, 40–42; LiDonnici, *Epidaurian Miracle Inscriptions*, 8–9; Flemming, 'Baths and Bathing', 23–32; and esp. Trümper, 'Bathing'. See also Griffith, 'Alternative Medicine'.

The water of this well 'is brought from a spot that is healthy and promotes health, inasmuch as it comes forth from the shrine and the feet of the Savior [τοῦ σωτῆρος].[39] For no water could flow from more healthful and purer places than that which flows from these' (39.6). The water from the sacred well of Asclepius 'is both sweet and fresh'. Moreover, it is so sweet that when one drinks it, one has no desire to add wine to it. Indeed, one will probably prefer the water to the wine (39.7). In fact, water from this well is never polluted nor depleted; time has no affect on it (39.9). The water from the god's well is 'not merely a drink, it is also a most pleasant bathing water that prevents harm' (39.12). The 'holy spring of Asclepius' (39.12) is the god's co-worker 'and it has often been useful to many in obtaining what they had asked from the god' (39.14). Bathing in this water has resulted in recovery of eyesight, the healing of 'ailments of the chest' and breathing problems. Indeed, we are told that one man, who was mute, regained his voice after drinking from the water of the well of Asclepius (39.15). This well water, says Aristides, is as Pindar 'pictured nectar: self-flowing, a potion blended sufficiently by some divine process of mixing' (39.16). The 'water is sacred because it saves those who use it', that is, those who drink it and bath in it (39.17). In view of this water's many benefits, Aristides can say that 'its patron god', Asclepius, 'is eminent among the gods' (39.18).[40]

We have an especially detailed testimony that makes frequent reference to curative and therapeutic bathing. At Epidaurus one Marcus Julius Apellas (c. 160 CE) inscribed a lengthy testimonial to his many treatments undertaken over an extended period of time.[41] Evidently most of his treatments, which often involved bathing, apparently were successful. Apellas, a priest from Idrias, suffered from sickness, which included indigestion, headaches, and sinus congestion. In a dream the god told him to go to the temple of Asclepius at Epidaurus. There he received directions regarding food, drink, and exercise. He was also instructed to wash himself without assistance, to sprinkle himself with sand, to walk barefoot, and before 'plunging into hot water, to pour wine over myself, (and) to bathe without help' (lines 12–13). Later Apellas is 'anointed all over with mustard and salt' (lines 17–18). He is then told, 'You are cured [τεθεράπευσαι], but you must pay the healing fees [ἴατρα]' (line 20). He bathed again and felt no pain (line 22). He remained at the temple and was told to use dill and olive oil to relieve his headaches, then gargle with something cold to relieve his sore throat (lines 26–31). The inscription ends: The god 'bade me also to inscribe this. Full of gratitude I departed well [ὑγιής]' (lines 31–33).

Skeptical of the alleged role of gods and demons, medical pioneer Hippocrates (fifth century BCE) nevertheless had much to say about the types and properties of water. Without making appeals to Asclepius or any other supernatural power, Hippocrates discusses 'waters, those that bring disease or very good health, and of the ill or good that is likely to arise from water. For the influence of water upon health is very great' (*De aere aquis et locis* 7.2–5). Hippocrates goes on to state which kinds of water are best for which kind of people and which kind of maladies. 'Rain waters are the lightest, sweetest, finest, and clearest ... Such waters are the best' (8.2, 49). 'Waters from snow and ice', however, 'are all bad. For, once frozen, water never recovers its original nature ...' (8.51). And finally, we are told that 'one water cannot be like another; some are sweet, others are impregnated with salt and alum ...' (9.9).[42]

---

39   Asclepius is often referred to as σωτήρ, but the god was given many appellations. For a list, see Walton, *Cult of Asklepios*, 83–84.
40   Translations of *Oratio* are adapted from Edelstein & Edelstein, *Asclepius*, 1:409–13.
41   *IG* IV² 1 no. 126 = *SIG* III no. 1170. The visit was for more than nine days, as indicated by lines 22–23 ('within nine days after I had come'), and 26 ('as I stayed on'). Apellas seems to have resided at the sanctuary for at least two weeks, perhaps longer.
42   Translations based on Jones, *Hippocrates I*, 83–95.

Although the science of Hippocrates is obviously naïve and erroneous at points, he does rightly recognize that certain waters are healthy (such as fresh rain water) and other waters are not (such as stagnant, turgid water). Here, too, the views of Hippocrates roughly coincide with the views of men like Aristides and Apellas who believed that healthy, curative water was provided by the gods, especially by Asclepius. Whatever their view of the gods, all agreed that good water was important for health. Of course, the majority of people in late antiquity would have been inclined to see the gods connected in one way or another with certain pools, springs, and wells. It was this general assumption that likely lay behind the glosses added to the Johannine story.

Besides water sources, Asclepian sanctuaries dedicated to healing usually had porticoes (στοαί) and it was within these open porticoes or sleep rooms (κοιμητήρια) called abatons (ἄβατα) that suppliants slept (καθεύδειν),[43] hoping for divine dreams and healing. Archaeological excavations at Epidaurus reveals a long portico that apparently housed a number of these abatons. Abatons are often mentioned in the Epidaurian testimonies.[44] Asclepian porticoes elsewhere are mentioned in the literature.

Near Corinth, Pausanias relates, is a sanctuary of Asclepius. Within it is a portico adorned with the figure called Sleep (*Hypnos*), an image of the 'Dream-god' (i.e., Asclepius), and other fixtures and images (*Graeciae descriptio* 2.10.2). In a nearby grove is a sanctuary dedicated to Hera. In it is a portico with wooden images of gods, but the image of Asclepius is made of stone (2.11.8). A contemporary Roman senator built a bath of Asclepius, which included a temple dedicated to Asclepius, his daughter Health (*Hygeia*), and Apollo. The senator also restored the portico (2.27.6).

John 5 and Asclepius?

Reference to the Asclepian porticoes brings us back to the Gospel of John. In a recent study Robin Thompson has taken a fresh look at the healing of the infirm man at the pool of Bethzatha/Bethesda in John 5. Given the description, especially the reference to the porticoes (στοαί) where the sick rest awaiting the agitation of the water, she wonders if the Johannine story was intended as a challenge to the Asclepian tradition.[45] Given the ambiguity and incompleteness of the archaeological excavations at Église Sainte-Anne, the probable first-century location of the pool, Thompson is unable to conclude that in the pre-70 era the pool was an Asclepian facility.[46] I find it hard to believe that a healing facility dedicated to a pagan deity could exist within pre-70 CE Jerusalem. This does not mean, however, that readers and hearers of the Johannine healing story would not have thought of the cult of Asclepius and would not have made comparisons between

---

43 Or 'slept in' (ἐνεκάθευδεν), that is, the suppliant slept *in the portico or in the abaton*, as in Arata's testimony (Epidaurus stele B lines 1–6), which was discussed above. In the play *Plutus* the character Chremylus advises a friend, with regard to the blind man, that they 'let him lie inside the temple of Asclepius the whole night long' (Aristophanes, *Plutus* 411). Asclepian sycophant Aristides dreamt of the temple of Asclepius in the gymnasium of Smyrna, finding it larger than expected, occupying 'all the levelled area of the stoa' (*Oratio* 47.17). The archaeological work undertaken at some of these sites has clarified the dimensions of the stoa and supporting structures.
44 LiDonnici, *Epidaurian Miracle Inscriptions*, 12–14. LiDonnici relies on Tomlinson, 'Two Buildings' and *Epidauros*.
45 See Thompson, 'Healing'.
46 In the aftermath of the destruction of the city in 70 CE, it is possible that columns that would have been part of the 'five porticoes' were salvaged and taken to new locations. Half of the site remains unexcavated, however, so the columns may still be present but not yet exposed. Another possibility is that the pool was remodeled as an Asclepieion clinic after the defeat of Bar Kokhba in 135 CE, when Jerusalem was rebuilt and renamed Aelia Capitolina and there was almost no Jewish population. The archaeological record is summed up in Thompson, 'Healing', 79–80.

Jesus the healer and Asclepius the healer. Many readers and hearers of the story probably did think of it as a challenge to the cult of Asclepius, as Thompson surmises.

We should also assume that some of the cities of the Decapolis, as well as one or two cities in the tetrarchy of Philip, son of Herod the Great, had buildings dedicated to the cult of Asclepius.[47] Caesarea Maritima, with its pro-Roman population, which included native Italians and legionnaires, is also a reasonable candidate. A half dozen sites in Israel have been identified as probably having a building and pool dedicated to Asclepius.[48] Accordingly, we should assume that the cult was nearby, if not present in Galilee in the Hellenistic and Roman periods and so would have been known to Jews in the land of Israel, just as the Asclepieia would have been known to Jews of the Diaspora.

There are a few specific details in the story of the lame man at the pool of Bethzatha/Bethesda that would have brought to mind the healing testimonies associated with Asclepius. First, the invalid awaits healing in the porticoes adjacent the pool. This was common in the Asclepian tradition. Second, the pool was believed to have curative powers when the water moved (perhaps moved by an angel). Waters with curative and therapeutic powers were also part of the Asclepian tradition. Third, Jesus asks the invalid, 'Do you wish to become well [ὑγιὴς γενέσθαι]?' (v. 6). The expression, ὑγιὴς γενέσθαι, is commonplace in the Asclepian testimonies. We saw an example above in the testimony of Nicanor the lame man. Fourth, Jesus instructs the man to get up, take up his pallet, and start walking (v. 8). In the Asclepian tradition the god often gives suppliants similar instructions. Fifth, the man obeys Jesus. He takes up his pallet and walks (v. 9). He is able to do this, because εὐθέως ἐγένετο ὑγιής, 'immediately he became well'. Again we have the language that is found in many of the Asclepian testimonies and we recall the instruction given to Hermodicos of Lampsacus above, who was told to 'carry into the sanctuary the biggest stone that he could' (Epidaurus stele A lines 108–9).

We find that the although the evidence is not sufficient to conclude that the pool of Bethzatha/Bethesda in the time of Jesus was part of an Asclepian healing center, or even in the later time when the evangelist composed his Gospel, it is very probable that most of those who read or heard this story would have compared it to Asclepian tradition and perhaps would have viewed Jesus as equal to, if not superior to the Greco-Roman god of healing.

Concluding Comments

Framing a healing story in such a way that intends readers to think of Asclepius should not surprise. By the time the Gospel of John was composed, the Jesus movement of Johannine circles was not only defending its faith in Jesus against the backdrop of a skeptical synagogue, it was trying to make the case in the pagan world that Jesus the crucified Jewish Messiah had more to offer than did the Greco-Roman gods, including the popular and trusted healing god Asclepius.

There could be intentional contrasts with Asclepian tradition elsewhere in the fourth Gospel. We may briefly consider a few. First, Jesus' appeal to Moses who lifted up the serpent (John 3:14–15; cf. Num 21:9) surely brought to mind the serpent of Asclepius, often depicted wrapped around

---

47 Caesarea Philippi, with its natural springs and many pagan temples, would have been ideally suited to the Asclepian cult.
48 For old study that is still worth reviewing, see McCasland, 'Asclepius Cult in Palestine'.

his staff (Ovid, *Metamorphoses* 15.58–62).⁴⁹ Secondly, the living waters Jesus provides (John 4:10–15; 7:38) probably made some readers/hearers think of the curative waters associated with Asclepius. Recall that Aelius Aristides claimed that the water from the well of Asclepius is 'sweet and fresh' and never depleted (*Oratio* 39.7–9). Third, it was when the mortal physician Asclepius managed to restore the life of a dead man, that jealous Zeus struck him dead with a lightning bolt, which in turn resulted in his apotheosis (Hesiod, *Fragmenta* 90; Aeschylus, *Agamemnon* 1019–1024; Euripides, *Alcestis* 127–129: 'for he [Asclepius] raised [ἀνίστη] (the dead), until the Zeus-flung fiery thunderbolt struck him').⁵⁰ A similar sequence is seen in the fourth Gospel, for it is after the resuscitation of Lazarus that the Jewish ruling priests determine that Jesus must die (John 11:45–53); and it is in death, in the 'lifting up' of Jesus on the cross, that Jesus returns to his Father in heaven (John 12:17–19, 23–24, 31–34).⁵¹

Fourth, Asclepius is addressed as 'true' (ἀληθινός). We have an interesting example in a magical text, probably dating from the second or third century, in which the supplicant is advised to petition the spiritual powers as follows: 'Send me the true Asclepius [τὸν ἀληθινὸν Ἀσκληπιόν], not some deceitful demon in place of the god [δίχα τινὸς ἀντιθέου πλανοδαίμονος]' (*PGM* VII.634–635). At the end of the charm, the supplicant is to cry out, 'Lord Asclepius, appear [κύριε Ἀσκληπιέ, φάνηθι]!' (VII.640–641).⁵² In the fourth Gospel Jesus is true, and his truth is in contrast to error. This is given expression in several ways. At the beginning of the Gospel the Logos, which takes up fleshly residence in Jesus, is said to be 'the true light [τὸ φῶς τὸ ἀληθινόν]' (John 1:9). He is 'full of grace and truth [πλήρης χάριτος καὶ ἀληθείας]' (1:14). Jesus tells the crowd that his 'Father gives you the true bread from heaven [τὸν ἄρτον ἐκ τοῦ οὐρανοῦ τὸν ἀληθινόν]' (6:32). Jesus goes on to say, 'For my flesh is true food [ἡ γὰρ σάρξ μου ἀληθής ἐστιν βρῶσις], and my blood is true drink [τὸ αἷμά μου ἀληθής ἐστιν πόσις]' (6:55). Indeed, the one who sent Jesus is 'true' (8:26 ὁ πέμψας με ἀληθής ἐστιν). Jesus is the 'truth' (14:6 ἐγώ εἰμι ἡ ὁδὸς καὶ ἡ ἀλήθεια καὶ ἡ ζωή). He is the 'true vine' (15:1 ἐγώ εἰμι ἡ ἄμπελος ἡ ἀληθινή). When he returns to his Father he will send 'the Spirit of truth' (15:26; 16:7 τὸ πνεῦμα τῆς ἀληθείας). He speaks 'the truth' (16:7 ἐγὼ τὴν ἀλήθειαν λέγω ὑμῖν). Jesus' mission is that people know the 'only true God [τὸν μόνον ἀληθινὸν θεόν]' (17:3).

The supplicant in the magical charm petitions the powers that 'the true Asclepius' be sent, not a 'deceitful demon' (πλανοδαίμων).⁵³ In the Gospel of John, Jesus the true light, the true bread, the true food, even the truth itself is accused of being possessed by a demon (7:20; 8:48 δαιμόνιον ἔχεις). The opponents of Jesus assert that Jesus' testimony is not true (8:13 ἡ μαρτυρία σου οὐκ ἔστιν ἀληθής). Unlike Jesus, they follow the lead of their 'father, the devil', in whom there is no truth, for he is 'a liar and father of lies' (8:44–45). The cynical Pontius Pilate, yielding to high-priestly pressure and probably viewed as a reflection of paganism, asks Jesus, 'What is truth

---

49 See the learned discussion in Charlesworth, *Good and Evil Serpent*, 360–414, 579–90 (notes). Snakes (ὄφις) or serpents (ὅρκων) are referenced in some of the healing testimonials (e.g., Epidaurus stele B lines 102–109; Epidaurus stele C lines 1–2). In the statuary of late antiquity Asclepius is often depicted with a serpent. For further discussion of the cults related to snakes and serpents, see Ogden, *Drakōn*. In early Christian art Jesus is often depicted holding a staff when performing a miracle or healing someone. The staff may owe its origin to Moses and his staff (or rod). This point is made in L. M. Jefferson, 'Jesus the Magician?'. There can be no doubt that the staff of Moses played an important part in the development of this motif, but I suspect comparison of Jesus with Asclepius did too.

50 Early Christian Fathers were very much aware of the apotheosis of Asclepius, both criticizing it and comparing it to the ascension and divinity of Jesus. See Theophilus, *Ad Autolycum* 1.13; Justin Martyr, *1 Apologia* 21.2; Athenagoras, *Legatio pro Christianis* 29.

51 Nicholson, *Death as Departure*.

52 For Greek text, see Preisendanz, *Papyri Graecae Magicae*, 2:29. The translation is mine, though one might wish to consult the translation and notes in Betz, *Greek Magical Papyri*, 136.

53 As we shall see, the πλανοδαίμων is the opposite of the ἀγαθὸς δαίμων.

[τί ἐστιν ἀλήθεια]?' (18:38). Of course, he expects no answer, for there is no truth. In the pagan world, the fourth evangelist implies, truth is unknown; and it will not be found in Asclepius or the other Greco-Roman deities.

Jesus and Asclepius are both referred to as 'good' (ἀγαθός). One will recall that when told of Jesus of Nazareth, Nathanael asks, 'Can anything good [τι ἀγαθόν] come out of Nazareth?' (John 1:46). Jesus demonstrates that he is indeed good, which is recognized by some of the crowd, who say of him, 'He is good [ἀγαθός]' (7:12). Asclepius was regarded as good, and sometimes was identified as the 'Good Daimon' (ὁ ἀγαθὸς δαίμων), in contrast to the aforementioned 'deceitful demon' (πλανοδαίμων). The Good Daimon appears often in the magical papyri, where he is described as joyful and holy.[54] In one Demotic-Greek text reference is made to 'him who is seated in the fiery cloak on the serpentine head of the Good Daimon [ἐπὶ τῆς ἀρουρέας κεφαλῆς τοῦ ἀγαθοῦ δαίμονος], the almighty, four-faced, highest daimon ....'[55] If 'serpentine' is the correct reading, then an allusion to Asclepius is probable.

The fourth Gospel may contain other contrasting allusions to Greco-Roman gods. An obvious possibility is the miracle at Cana of Galilee, where Jesus changed the water into wine (John 2:1–11). We find numerous references to Dionysus creating wine for humans (e.g., Euripides, *Bacchae* 534–536, 651, 704–711,[56] 769–774; Ps.-Apollodorus, *Bibliotheca* 3.14.7 'Icarios ... received from Dionysus a branch of a vine and learned how to make wine'; Diodorus Siculus, *Bibliotheca Historica* 3.62.5; Plutarch, *Lysander* 28.4; Athenaeus, Deipnosophistae 1.26; Aelian, *Varia historia* 3.41). Greek novelist Achilles Tatius (early second century?) reminds his readers of the old story in which Dionysius turns water into wine to thank a shepherd who had showed him hospitality. Amazed by the drink, the shepherd asks the god, 'Where, stranger, did you find this water stained with red?' Dionysius replied, 'This is the water, and this is the fountain' (*Leucippe et Cleitophon* 2.2.1–6).[57]

Christian fathers know the myth, of course, and make reference to it. Athenagoras, for example, calls Dionysus the 'fruit of the vine [ἀμπέλου καρπόν]' (*Legatio pro Christianis* 22), while Justin Martyr reminds Trypho that pagans say that Dionysus 'was the discoverer of wine [εὑρετὴν ἀμπέλου γενόμενον]' (*Dialogos cum Tryphone* 69.2; cf. *1 Apologia* 54.6). Athanasius asserts that 'Dionysus is worshipped among them because he has taught humankind drunkenness' (*De incarnatione* 49.3). He adds that the people of India use the name of Dionysus as a 'symbol for

---

54 This ubiquitous spirit or genius, appears often in magical texts and other literature. In Egyptian texts the ἀγαθὸς δαίμων is usually in reference to various Egyptian deities, though the sobriquet was also applied to Greco-Roman deities, such as Apollo and Asclepius. For examples in the *Papyri Graecae Magicae*, see IV.1609 ('Come to me, joyful Good Daimon [ὁ ἱλαρὸς ἀγαθὸς δαίμων]'), 3169 ('O Holy Good Daimon [ἱερὲ ἀγαθὲ δαίμων]'); VII.492–493 (the Good Daimon [ὁ ἀγαθὸς δαίμων] permits Isis to rule); XII.134–135 ('Listen to me, you also, O Good Daimon [ἀγαθὲ δαίμων], whose might is very great among the gods'); XIII.770 (appeal is made to ὁ ἀγαθὸς δαίμων).

55 For text (which here is Greek), see Griffith & Thompson, *Demotic Magical Papyrus*, 42. With respect to ἀρουρέας, Griffith & Thompson admit to being uncertain, both with regard to the reading and to the meaning. In Betz (ed.), *The Greek Magical Papyri in Translation*, 201, it is understood as 'serpentine'. In Betz the passage is cited as *Papyri Demoticae Magicae* xiv.108–109, while in Griffith and Thompson it is IV.15–17. For examples of art at Pompeii depicting snakes, Asclepius, and Good Daimon, see Charlesworth, *Good and Evil Serpent*, 102 (fig. 36), 465 (fig. 92). A stele with Greek and Latin inscriptions depicts a bearded figure (probably Asclepius) and a snake. Both Asclepius and the ἀγαθὸς δαίμων are mentioned. For description and discussion, see G. Ferrari, *Il commercio dei sarcofagi asiatici* (Studia Archeologica 7; Rome: 'L'Erma' di Bretschneider, 1966), 20.

56 Lines 704–707: 'Someone grasped a thyrsus and struck it into a rock from which a dewy stream of water [δροσώδης ὕδατος] leaps out; another struck her rod on the ground and for her the god sent up a spring of wine [τῇδε κρήνην ἐξανῆκ' οἴνου θεός]'. Translation based on Kirk, *The Bacchae*, 82.

57 Bowersock, *Fiction as History*, 125–26. Bowersock suspects that Achilles Tatius has modified the Dionysus myth so as to echo the Christian tradition of the Words of Institution in which Jesus identifies the wine with his blood.

wine' (*Contra gentes* 24.2). The Clementine *Homilies* link the 'cloudy vapors' (ἀτμῶν θολεράν) of drunkenness with Dionysius (*Homiliae Clementinae* 6.9.3).

The fourth Gospel is rightly and primarily understood in the context of conflict with a synagogue that has come to reject the Christian confession and to remove from its membership those who make this confession (cf. John 9:22; 12:42; 16:2). But the fourth Gospel was also composed to offer, it seems to me, an implicit critique of elements of pagan mythology. For the Christian Church to make headway against pagan skepticism and persecution, it is necessary to demonstrate that the advantages of faith in Jesus the crucified and resurrected Son of God, who healed and raised the dead and whose followers continue his ministry in his name, outweigh the advantages of faith in the Olympian gods, above all the healing god Asclepius. The fourth evangelist seems to have made an attempt to do this.

Bibliography

Avalos, H. *Health Care and the Rise of Christianity* (Peabody: Hendrickson, 1999).

Bittner, W.J. *Jesu Zeichen im Johannesevangelium: Die Messias-Erkenntnis im Johannesevangelium vor ihrem jüdische Hintergrund* (WUNT II/26; Tübingen: Mohr Siebeck, 1987).

Berger, K. *Im Anfang war Johannes: Datierung und Theologie des vierten Evangeliums* (Stuttgart: Quell, 1997).

Betz, H.D. (ed.) *The Greek Magical Papyri in Translation, Including the Demotic Spells: Volume One: Texts* (2nd ed., Chicago: The University of Chicago Press, 1992).

Bowersock, G.W. *Fiction as History: Nero to Julian* (Sather Classical Lectures 58; Berkeley: University of California Press, 1994).

Carson, D.A. *The Gospel according to John* (Grand Rapids: Eerdmans, 1991).

Chadwick, H. *Origen: Contra Celsum* (Cambridge: Cambridge University Press, 1953).

Charlesworth, J.H. *The Good and Evil Serpent* (New Haven: Yale University Press, 2010).

Cotter, W.J. 'Miracles Stories: The God Asclepius, the Pythagorean Philosophers, and the Roman Rulers', in D. C. Allison Jr., J. D. Crossan, & A. J. Levine (eds.), *The Historical Jesus in Context* (Princeton Readings in Religions; Princeton and Oxford: Princeton University Press, 2006), 166–78.

Donnegan, J. *A New Greek and English Lexicon* (London: Bohn, 1846).

Edelstein, E.J., & L. Edelstein *Asclepius: Collection and Interpretation of the Testimonies* (vols. 1 and 2; Baltimore and London: The Johns Hopkins University Press, 1945).

Ensor, P.W. *Jesus and His 'Works': The Johannine Sayings in Historical Perspective* (WUNT II/85; Tübingen: Mohr Siebeck, 1996).

Ferrari, G. *Il commercio dei sarcofagi asiatici* (Studia Archeologica 7; Rome: 'L'Erma' di Bretschneider, 1966).

Flemming, R.	'Baths and Bathing in Greek Medicine', in S.K. Lucore & M. Trümper (eds.), *Greek Baths and Bathing Culture: New Discoveries and Approaches* (Babesch Sup. 23; Leuven: Peeters, 2013), 23–32.
Griffith, A.B.	'Alternative Medicine in Pre-Roman and Republican Italy: Sacred Springs, Curative Baths and "Votive Religion"', in C. Krotzl, K. Mustakallio, & J. Kuuliala (eds.), *Infirmity in Antiquity and the Middle Ages: Social and Cultural Approaches to Health, Weakness and Care* (Farnham: Ashgate, 2015), 185–200.
Griffith, F.L., & H. Thompson (eds.)	*The Demotic Magical Papyrus of London and Leiden* (London: Grevel, 1904).
Jefferson, L.M.	'Jesus the Magician? Why Jesus Holds a Wand in Early Christian Art', *BAR* 46.4 (2020), 41–47.
Jeremias, J.	'λίθος, λίθινος', *TDNT* 4.268–280.
Jones, W.H.S.	*Hippocrates I* (LCL 147; Cambridge MA: Harvard University Press, 1923).
Kirk, G.S.	*The Bacchae by Euripides: A Translation with Commentary* (Englewood Cliffs NJ: Prentice-Hall, 1970).
Lake, K.	*Eusebius Ecclesiastical History I* (LCL 153; London: Heinemann; Cambridge, MA: Harvard University Press, 1926).
Lee, T.R.	*Studies in the Form of Sirach 44–50* (SBLDS 75; Atlanta: Scholars Press, 1986).
LiDonnici, L.R.	*The Epidaurian Miracle Inscriptions: Text, Translation and Commentary* (SBLTT 36; GRR 11; Atlanta: Scholars Press, 1995).
McCasland, S.V.	'The Asclepius Cult in Palestine', *JBL* 58 (1939), 221–27.
Metzger, B.M.	*A Textual Commentary on the Greek New Testament* (London and New York: United Bible Societies, 1975).
Minns, D., & P. Parvis	*Justin, Philosopher and and Martyr: Apologies* (Oxford Early Christian Texts; Oxford: Oxford University Press, 2009).
Nicholson, G.C.	*Death as Departure: The Johannine Descent-Ascent Schema* (SBLDS 63; Chico: Scholars Press, 1983).
Obermann, A.	*Die christologische Erfüllung der Schrift im Johannesevangelium* (WUNT II.83; Tübingen: Mohr Siebeck, 1996).
Ogden, D.	*Drakōn: Dragon Myth and Serpent Cult in the Greek and Roman Worlds* (Oxford: Oxford University Press, 2013).
Preisendanz, K. (ed.)	*Papyri Graecae Magicae: Die Griechischen Zauberpapyri* (2 vols., Leipzig: B. G. Teubner, 1928–31; rev. ed., 1973; repr. Munich and Leipzig: K. G. Saur, 2001).
Reich, R., E. Shukron, & O. Lernau	'Recent Discoveries in the City of David, Jerusalem,' *IEJ* 57 (2007), 153–68.

Reitzenstein, R. — *Die Hellenistischen Mysterienreligionen: nach ihren Grundgedanken und Wirkungen* (2nd ed., Leipzig and Berlin: B. G. Teubner, 1920).

Remus, H. — *Pagan-Christian Conflict over Miracle in the Second Century* (Patristic Monograph Series 10; Cambridge, MA: The Philadelphia Patristic Foundation, 1983).

Rengstorf, K.H. — 'ἀποστέλλω (πέμπω), ἐξαποστέλλω, ἀπόστολος, ψευδαπόστολος, ἀποστολή', *TDNT* 1.398–447.

Roberts, A., & J. Donaldson (eds.) — *The Ante-Nicene Fathers* (10 vols., Edinburgh: T&T Clark, 1898).

Shanks, H. — 'The Siloam Pool Where Jesus Cured the Blind Man', *BAR* 31/5 (Sept-Oct 2005), 16–23.

Shemesh, A.O. — 'Therapeutic Bathing in Rabbinic Literature: Halachic Issues and their Background in History and Realia', *Jewish Medical Ethics* 7/2 (2010), 57–67.

Smith, D.M. — *Johannine Christianity* (Columbia: University of South Carolina Press, 1984).

Thompson, R. — 'Healing at the Pool of Bethesda: A Challenge to Asclepius?', *BBR* 27 (2017), 65–84.

Tomlinson, R.A. — *Epidauros* (Austin: University of Texas Press, 1983).

Tomlinson, R.A. — 'Two Buildings in Sanctuaries of Asklepios', *JHS* 89 (1969), 106–17.

Trümper, M. — 'Bathing in the Sanctuaries of Asklepios and Apollo Maleatas at Epidauros', in A. Avramidou & D. Demetriou (eds.), *Approaching the Ancient Artifact: Representation, Narrative, and Function. A Festschrift in Honor of H. Alan Shapiro* (Berlin: de Gruyter, 2014), 211–31.

von Wahlde, U.C. — 'The Pool of Siloam: The Importance of the New Discoveries for Our Understanding of Ritual Immersion in Late Second Temple Judaism and the Gospel of John', in P.N. Anderson, F. Just, & T. Thatcher (eds.), *John, Jesus, and History. Vol. 2: Aspects of Historicity in the Fourth Gospel* (Society of Biblical Literature Early Christianity and its Literature 2; Atlanta: Society of Biblical Literature, 2009), 155–73.

Walton, A. — *The Cult of Asklepios* (Cornell Studies in Classical Philology 3; Boston: Ginn, 1894).

Young, F.W. — 'A Study of the Relation of Isaiah to the Fourth Gospel', *ZNW* 46 (1955), 215–33.

Craig A. Evans
Houston Baptist University

"When they heard this, they were silenced" (Acts 11:18)
Some Inner-Christian Conflicts and Their Resolution in Acts 6–15:35

CHRISTOPH STENSCHKE

Abstract

This chapter builds on W. Mayer's reminder that the current focus on conflict and violence in popular and academic studies of religious conflict must not detract from instances of de-escalation and resolution of conflict. In view of this, the paper examines the origin, the contested domains and enabling conditions, as well as the de-escalation and resolution of some of the inner-Christian conflicts in the Book of Acts (6:1–7; 11:1–18; 15:1–35). How is resolution of conflict achieved and the unity of the community retained? What kinds of resource are available to the community for resolving its conflicts? The final section reflects on how this portrayal can be applied to inner-Christian and other conflicts in the present day-world.

Introduction

For a number of reasons, most of them sad and disturbing, religious conflict has become a dominant theme in religious studies during the past few years.[1] This quest is part of a larger, interdisciplinary interest in violence.[2] The Book of Acts contains conflicts of all sorts. It offers a multifactorial portrayal of religious conflict of different types, including a number of conflicts within the Christian communities of Jerusalem and Antioch.[3]

Before turning to the conflict and resolution accounts of Acts, we first refer to a number of issues in the excellent survey of the current discussion of religious conflict by Australian scholar Wendy Mayer.[4] Concerning the range of issues involved, she argues that religious conflict:

> encompasses not just the physical domain (violent acts), but also the discursive (violent, i.e., hostile/hate-filled speech),

---

[1] For a convenient survey of recent contributions see, Mayer, 'Religious Conflict', 1; on religion and violence in general, see Juergensmeyer, Kitts & Jerryson, Handbook.
[2] For a survey, see Gudehus & Christ, Gewalt.
[3] Conflicts among Christians are not mentioned for other places. See, however, discussion on Acts 20:29–30 below.
[4] Mayer, 'Religious Conflict'.

raising questions about the precise relationship between these two forms, how each should be addressed, and the degree to which each is harmful to society. The motivation for such violence, moreover, is often complex, leading to the conclusion, on the one hand, that violent "religious" conflicts in late antiquity, for instance, were rarely purely religiously motivated. On careful examination they can be shown to owe as much, if not more, to political considerations, local conditions, and the personal motives of the chief protagonists.[5]

Mayer emphasises the need for careful definition of the concept of religious conflict. She suggests that:

> religious conflict is best described as a more complex phenomenon that engages a combination of contested domains, including power, personality, space or place, and group identity. These contested domains should not be confused with enabling factors or conditions, which … can be political, social, economic, cultural and psychological. When both of these aspects are taken into consideration, we should be open to the possibility that, as a religion develops over time and/or as different enabling conditions come into play, different contested domains are accorded priority. A distinction should also be drawn between the root cause/s of the religious conflict (what is contested) and the way in which the conflict is discursively or narratively framed. That is, what a conflict is said to be about may differ significantly from what is actually being contested. We should be similarly open to the possibility that what is contested may be reframed retrospectively, just as it is also possible that what is not a conflict becomes viewed or framed as a conflict in hindsight and vice versa.[6]

Two further issues need clarification in defining religious conflict, namely the agents involved and what precisely identifies a conflict as *religious*. Mayer explains:

> While individuals may be the chief protagonists, the coupling of religion with conflict implies that the agents involved are not individuals, but collective individuals, i.e., groups or communities. … the agents in religious conflict are two or more groups that derive from identifiably separate religions, separate factions within the same religion (that result from splintering, i.e., sectarianism), the same faction within a religion (where splintering has not yet occurred – and may or may not, in fact, eventuate), and secular authority, the latter of which may also wield religious authority.[7]

These observations are important for the inner-Christian conflicts of Acts. Their protagonists are either groups of people or individuals. However, the individuals 'self-identify and operate as part of a larger system', namely, the apostolic band and/or the Jerusalem Christian community. All figures are firmly rooted in the Christian community and this community at large is involved in these conflicts to different extents.

The question of what identifies a conflict as religious depends on how one defines religion and also determines how broadly or narrowly the investigation is focused. Mayer argues for a definition that is not restrictive. Accordingly, conflict is *religious*:

> when a conflict occurs in which religion is also involved. This avoids questions of

---

5 Mayer, 'Religious Conflict', 1–2. Mayer describes the theoretical approaches that have been used in recent decades, including discussion of a number of significant research projects on ancient religious conflicts (pp.5–14). Mayer's survey includes the instructive *Religious Rivalries Seminar*, which was conducted under the auspices of the Canadian Society of Biblical Studies.

6 Mayer, 'Religious Conflict', 3.
7 Mayer, 'Religious Conflict', 4.

the nature: when is a conflict religious and when is it political/ethnic, since it allows that a conflict can be both. It also avoids questions about degree, that is, whether a conflict is primarily religious or primarily political/ethnic, since under this definition all conflicts are religious in which, whether in large degree or small, religion is involved.

To sum up, then, for the purposes of studying this phenomenon in as open a way as possible, religious conflict can be said to occur when the following conditions are satisfied:

1) two or more collective agents are involved and the agents derive, for example, from separate religions, separate factions within the same religion, from within the same faction in the same religion, and/or secular authority;
2) a domain – e.g., ideology/morality, power, personality, space/place, group identity – is contested, singly or in combination;
3) there are enabling conditions – e.g., political, social, economic, cultural and psychological; and
4) religion is involved (the degree to which it is involved is deemed irrelevant).[8]

In the inner-Christian conflicts of Acts, religious issues are clearly involved. The agents derive from 'separate factions within the same religion', that is, different Christian factions within Judaism or from within the same faction (Jewish Christians) in the same religion (that is, Judaism). The analysis will show to what extent Mayer's distinction between contested domains and enabling conditions will prove helpful in our analysis.

Mayer also observes that in the recent discussion of religious conflict:

> the *focus on violence* (one extreme of religious conflict) obscures broader questions about what occurs *before or apart from violence*: the mechanisms at play in how conflict originates in the first instance, how it manifests in its early stages, the phenomenon of splintering into sub-groups (sectarianism) within a religion, and precisely what factors are operative in conflict escalation and de-escalation.[9]

In contrast to other conflicts in Acts, the inner-Christian conflicts do not involve violence. Although sharp disagreement is not passed over in silence, there is no violence. Therefore, in view of Mayer's observations, we focus on the 'broader questions' and examine the portrayal of 'what occurs before or apart from *violence*', the origins of conflict and its manifestations in early stages, the contested domains and enabling conditions and the factors operative in the de-escalation and resolution of conflict.[10] Once the conflicts have been resolved, Acts paints a picture of peaceful *co-existence* and *co-operation* of the former conflict parties. This portrayal suggests some measure of *transition* and *assimilation* to the consensus which was reached.[11] In short, we will apply a number of insights of recent theorising on religious conflict to Acts in order to shed fresh light on the inner-Christian conflicts.

Some introductory observations are in order:

– In this study we concentrate on the *literary portrayal* of religious conflict. I do not discuss the historical validity of this portrayal[12] or its contribution to the

---

8   Mayer, *'Religious Conflict',* 5.

9   Mayer, *'Religious Conflict',* 19; italics mine.

10 Mayer, *'Religious Conflict',* 18 rightly cautions that the focus on religious conflict and violence must not detract from instances of conflict de-escalation and conflict resolution, which also appear in Acts.

11 See Mayer, *'Religious Conflict',* 17.

12 Mayer, 'Religious Conflict', 15 also points to the 'perennial issue of the bias of the surviving sources, and the historical forces that led to the transmission of some and the suppression or dwindling into obscurity of others'. For a recent survey of the issues and debate, see Keener, *Acts I,* 90–220 and Frey, Rothschild & Schröter, *Apostelgeschichte.* The approach taken in my study of the portrayal of translocal links between early Christian communities in Acts should be helpful in this regard; see Stenschke, 'Apostel'.

reconstruction of early Christian history.
- We focus only on conflicts involving the *whole community*, at least as *one* of the parties in conflict and resolution. While we include the conflict of Peter with a subgroup of the community of Jerusalem in Acts 11:1–18 ('the circumcision party', 11:2), we do *not* include the conflict of Peter with Ananias and Sapphira in Acts 5:1–11, as it is not community conflict as such.[13] There is no de-escalation or resolution to the conflict of Acts 5. Ananias and Sapphira remain in hypocrisy and lies.

They do not repent and are not given an opportunity to do so (in contrast to other figures in Acts).[14] Both of them die under divine judgement. They are not reconciled to God, to Peter or to the community of believers. Of all the conflict accounts in Acts, this is the only conflict in which Satan and the Holy Spirit are involved.

- Primarily, Acts is not a book about conflict and as such it is not a handbook on conflict de-escalation and resolution. If we make these issues our focus in this study, we need to be aware that we are asking questions which the author of Acts is not seeking to answer.[15]

- In our discussion of the *de-escalation and resolution of conflict* rather than the common Christian concept of reconciliation,[16] we follow the terminology of studies of religious conflict as indicated above. In addition, the language of reconciliation hardly occurs in Acts. The one and only occurrence of the technical terminology of reconciliation in Acts appears in Stephen's survey of the history of Israel in Acts 7.[17] Stephen mentions Moses' attempt of mediating between two quarrelling Israelites: "And on the following day, Moses appeared to them as they were quarrelling and tried to *reconcile them to peace*, saying: 'Men, you are brothers. Why do you wrong each other?'" (v. 26, καὶ συνήλλασεν αὐτοὺς εἰς εἰρήνην). This occurrence shows that the author

---

13 See the detailed treatment in Keener, *Acts II*, 1183–1197. Because it is a conflict between an individual and the community, I have not included the tension between Saul and the community of Jerusalem after his return from Damascus (9:26–30): 'all were afraid of him, for they did not believe that he was a disciple' (9:26). In addition, those reluctant to receive Paul questioned whether Paul has actually become part of the Christian community. Acts does not indicate how the believer dealt with Saul's past activities once he was accepted into the community.
   Inner-Christian conflicts involving Paul's actual or alleged activities as an individual also appear in Acts 19:30–31; 21:4, 12–14 and 21:20–26; on Acts 19:30–31 see Thompson, 'Unity', 537–538, for Acts 21:1–14 see pp. 538–539. Recalling the conflict in Acts 11:1–18 between Peter (as an individual) and the believers in Jerusalem in several ways, Acts 21:20–26 reports a latent conflict between large numbers of Jewish Christians in Jerusalem ('how many thousands there are among the Jews of those who have believed. They are all zealous for the law', 21:20) and Paul as an individual. It is an *indirect* conflict over Paul's own loyalty to his Jewish identity (see 11:2–3) and his ministry *among Jews* in the Diaspora. There is no open conflict: the leaders of the community tell Paul about the suspicions of many Jewish Christians in Jerusalem against him and suggest a plan of action for disproving and dispelling these reservations. There is no direct encounter between Paul and those suspicious of him or open criticism. The solution envisaged is not a verbal defence or a lengthy verbal interaction as in Acts 11 and 15, but involve actions intended to demonstrate Paul's own loyalty to Judaism and to disprove rumours about him. Acts 21:20–26 is often taken as Luke's acknowledgement of disagreement between Paul and the Jerusalem elders. For the inner-Christian conflict narratives of Acts, see also Cullmann, 'Dissensions'; Roloff, 'Konflikte'; Goulder, *St. Paul*; and Rakotoharintsifa, 'Luke'.

14 The case could be argued that Peter does not act as a private person but as the leader of the group of the apostles or as leader of the community. He acts with their approval.

15 Recent commentaries on Acts are Peterson, *Acts*; Schnabel, *Acts*; Haacker, *Apostelgeschichte*; Jennings, *Acts*; Keener, *Acts I–III*.

16 For a survey see Yarbrough, 'Forgiveness and Reconciliation', 502.

17 See Keener, *Acts II*, 1393–1394. There is no occurrence of this terminology in Acts with regard to reconciliation between God and people as in Pauline literature.

of Acts is aware of this terminology, but has not employed it anywhere else, for instance, in the context of the resolution of inner-Christian conflicts.[18]

I. Inner-Christian conflicts in Acts and their resolution

The beginning of Acts offers a portrayal of an ideal community of Christ-believers in Jerusalem (2:42–47; 4:32–37). They share goods and there is great unity among the believers[19] in contrast to the various groups within Judaism and the inhabitants of Jerusalem (the people, the religious leaders).

However, as the conflict accounts of Acts 6:1–6; 11:1–18; and 15:1–35 indicate, this portrayal of the early Christian community in Jerusalem is not without challenges.[20] In our study of each of these conflicts we draw on Mayer's insights on recent theorising about religious conflict and employ the same pattern, where applicable. After a brief summary of the *occasion* of the conflict, we examine the *contested domains* (what the conflict is about) and *enabling conditions* in each conflict (the resources available to the parties to the conflict and which are employed and which make conflict possible) and measures taken to initiate *de-escalation* and the *resolution* of conflict. In closing we ask whether the solution was persistent.

II.1. Acts 6:1–7: Neglect of a sub-group

The enigmatic summary in Acts of the *occasion* of the first inner-community conflict is a complaint by the 'Hellenists' (Jewish Christians with a Diaspora- Jewish background[21]), against the 'Hebrews' (Jewish Christians from Jerusalem or Judea). They complained because the widows of the Hellenist faction were being neglected in the daily distribution (of food or money to obtain it). As the distribution was up to that point the apostles' responsibility (themselves Judeans), the complaint should have been directed against them. Acts does not indicate why this was not the case,[22] neither is there any indication whether the complaint was justified or whether the neglect of the widows was more a matter of perception than real. Compared to the conflict of the apostles with the religious leadership of Jerusalem in Acts 4–5, the account of this first inner-community conflict is short and its course 'mild' (no violence or threats of violence).

The *contested domains* are on first sight financial means which were unevenly distributed and of which a needy group of people (widows) in the community was deprived. One can only speculate whether other issues were contested as well, such as those relating to culture and language,[23] the identity of the community, lack of attention by the

---

18 Perhaps this was the case as the attempt of Moses failed. The simple verb ἀλλάσσω appears in Acts 6:14 in the sense of *altering*, 'change the customs that Moses delivered to us'.
19 For a recent detailed analysis see Thompson, *One Lord*, 57–104, and Hume, *Early Christian Community*.
20 The account of the death of Ananias and Sapphira in Acts 5:1–11 indicates that the sharing of goods was not without challenges.
21 For their identity, see Zugmann, *Hellenisten*.
22 Did this happen out of reverence for the apostles? Were people slow to criticise them after the Ananias and Sapphira incident or the stunning miracles of Acts 5? In most of Acts 4–5, the apostles were engaged in conflict with the religious leaders of Jerusalem. This would have affected their responsibilities within the Christian community.
23 For a survey of possible issues see Keener, *Acts II*, 1253–1260. Possibly, the complaining of the 'Hellenists' was an expression of a more fundamental disagreement or estrangement from the 'Hebrews'.

apostles and their authority in the community.[24] Does the neglect of some and the reaction to it perhaps point to the issue of equality within the people of God?

Enabling conditions do not play a major role in this conflict. The Hellenists 'complain'. In this way, the disadvantaged party draws attention to an existing and pressing problem. The Greek word for this activity, γογγυσμός — recalls the repeated *murmuring* of Israel against Moses (and indirectly against God) during their desert wanderings.[25] They do not employ one or more of the other means which appear in the conflict accounts of Acts. The enabling condition on the side of the apostles is their ability to summon the full number of disciples and to address them. They can also trust that the disciples will follow their instruction by electing suitable people and presenting these people to them. Apparently there are enough suitable and willing people available. Prior to this conflict, the apostles receive full recognition from the whole community. They are furthermore portrayed as faithfully obeying the commission given to them by Jesus despite suffering, and as divinely affirmed through exceptional miracles—both within and outside of the community.

The *de-escalation* of this conflict starts with the initiative of the apostles. They do not ignore the situation or the complaint. Instead, they call *the whole community* together (6:2) to remind the people of the particular task given to them as apostles and insist that they cannot (or can no longer) 'serve tables' instead. The apostles trust the assembled community and propose that seven people be elected by the community for this task and indicate their qualifications (6:3). The apostles will then stick to their particular calling. 'And what they said pleased *the whole gathering*'. As a result, the entire community chooses seven men who fulfil the criteria outlined previously. These men make themselves available. All seven men bear Greek names. Presumably they come from the group of the Hellenists. Apparently they were trusted that they would not neglect the Hebrew widows either. These men were brought to the apostles and ordained to this task. This was a public act. It was clear to the whole community who is now entrusted with 'serving tables'. Thompson comments: 'The interplay of a proposal by the Twelve, the choice of seven by "the whole community", the presentation of the Seven to the apostles and the final ratification of the decision by the apostles is a model of harmonious cooperation'.[26] Acts 6:1–7 does not report the consequences of this conflict for the community.[27] Presumably the men fulfilled their task and the complaints stopped. The unity— which was emphasised previously—was restored.

According to the portrayal of Acts, the solution to this conflict was persistent (or, at least, Acts does not report further conflicts between these parties). The accounts of further inner-Christian conflicts (see below) do not mention these groups again,[28] nor are there further instances of complaints against each other or neglect of particularly vulnerable groups.[29]

---

24 See Thompson, *One Lord*, 93–96. Thompson argues that the widows, as the people at the centre of the conflict, indicate that the passage concerns the fulfilment of the Law's injunctions to provide for widows. In addition, the emphasis is on 'the unity of the Christian community under the chosen leadership of the Lord Jesus – the apostles' (p.93). Therefore the conflict was not a disagreement over a mere practical issue but over a matter of theological importance (p.95): 'The narrative cotext indicates that, for Luke, this dispute has the potential to threaten the life of the church (this time the threat is another internal threat in the cotext of increasing external threats'.
25 See Keener, *Acts II*, 1261–1262; Keener also surveys other intertextual links to Numbers 11.
26 Thompson, *One Lord*, 96.
27 Acts 6:7 notes: 'And the word of God continued to increase and the number of disciples multiplied greatly in Jerusalem, and a great many of the priests became obedient to the faith'.
28 Possibly conflicts between Hebrews and Hellenists lie behind the conflicts in Acts 15:1–35 and 21:18–26.
29 This may be due to the fact that the Hellenists had to flee from Jerusalem after the death of Stephen, one of the seven appointed men.

II.2. Acts 11:1–18: Re-negotiating Jewish identity

In the portrayal of Acts, the *occasion* of this second round of conflict is the fact that Peter went to the Gentiles in Caesarea and ate with them (11:3; the account of his activities is given in Acts 10:1–48). The events in Caesarea become known in Jerusalem: 'Now the apostles and brothers who were throughout Judea heard that the Gentiles had received the word of God'. On his return to Jerusalem, Peter is challenged by the 'circumcision party' ('those of the circumcision', 11:2), who were not privy to the course of the events. Regarding their identity, Schnabel notes:

> Since their critique does not mention the need to circumcise the converted Gentiles, they are evidently not identical with the "circumcision group" of Gal 2:12 …, nor are they identical with the minority group in the Jerusalem church consisting of converted Pharisees who later demanded that Gentile converts be circumcised (Acts 15:5). The expression "the circumcised believers" describes Jewish believers who, as Jews, obviously were circumcised, in contrast to the converted Gentiles (…, v. 1), who were not.[30]

This group criticises Peter for going to Gentiles (presumably, for entering their ritually unclean houses) and for eating with them (unclean food).[31]

As in the case of the complaint against the 'Hebrews' (when actually the apostles were responsible, not the 'Hebrews'), one may ask whether Peter's own transgression of Jewish purity laws was the real issue in this conflict. In doing so, Peter surely relativised important aspects of Jewish identity (addressed in detail in Acts 10:9–16). In the background was the issue of including Gentiles *as Gentiles* into the people of God, *which led to such problematic table-fellowship: had they become proper Law-abiding Jewish proselytes, the problem would not have arisen.* The vague accusation of 'going to Gentiles' and the unexpected interference in Acts 11:18 may suggest that the conflict also concerned the manner of including Gentiles: the critics do not explicitly agree that Peter was right in going to Gentiles and eating with them, but conclude from his report that God has granted to the Gentiles as well, repentance that leads to life.

As the account stands, the *contested domain* in this conflict is the necessity of Jewish Christians to adhere to Jewish purity regulations and all that is related to such regulations. For those of the 'circumcision party', this was mandatory and the significance of the Law was non-negotiable. From the account of Acts 10 and Peter's response, it becomes clear that he initially shared the position of his critics and staunchly defended it. Peter, however, had to change his mind due to divine intervention. There is no indication that the authority of Peter as such, or his leadership role in the community, was challenged. The charge of transgressing purity regulations would have discredited him indirectly.

Like with the first conflict, the *enabling condition* on the side of the opponents is the verbal criticism of Peter. However, the enabling condition on Peter's side is his trustworthy account of divine preparation and initiative in the events. Peter did not act of his own volition—rather, he reluctantly but obediently followed divine prompting. Therefore, one could almost say that if anyone, then God is to be blamed. Peter also mentions six witnesses to at least some of the events (11:12). As such, his account is trustworthy and stands up to scrutiny. As a witness of the life and teaching of Jesus, he can refer to words of Jesus (11:16). In addition, Peter received tremendous divine affirmation through his miracles, immediately prior to the

---

30 Schnabel, *Acts*, 508; similarly Thompson, *One Lord*, 100. This unusual designation, rather than 'the disciples' as elsewhere in the early chapters of Acts, emphasises their Jewish identity vis-à-vis the new Gentile believers.

31 For Jewish purity concerns and regulations, see Keener, *Acts II*, 1819–1821, 1777–1778.

disputed events (healing paralyzed Aeneas in Lydda and raising Tabitha from the dead in Joppa, 9:32–43) and later through his miraculous liberation from prison in Acts 12:3–19.

Again, the course of this second conflict is mild (in comparison to the previous conflict of Stephen with some of the Diaspora Jews and the ensuing persecution of Christians, and compared to the fate suffered by Paul in Damascus and in Jerusalem).

Peter takes his critics seriously and he is ready to be held accountable. The process of *de-escalation* is initiated through Peter's detailed account of the events in good order, which preceded his disputed behaviour and which explains the reason for his change in attitude and behaviour (11:5–17). Peter summarises the events of chapter 10 and emphasises the *divine interventions* in the process. He first mentions the vision which challenged not only his own attitude but also that of his critics (11:5–10): 'What God has made clean, do not call common' (11:9). He also refers to the divine command to go along with the envoys of Cornelius ('And the Spirit told me to go with them, making no distinction', 11:12). Only because of such prompting did Peter enter a Gentile house. If he wanted to be obedient (which is mandatory to do when the Spirit prompts—see 5:32), Peter had no choice but to go to uncircumcised men, as he was charged (11:3).

Peter mentions six Christians who came with him and served as witnesses of the event (11:12). Then Peter quotes verbatim the message which Cornelius received from an angel who commanded him to summon Peter (11:13). He indicates the significance of this encounter: 'he will declare to you a message by which you will be saved, you and all your household' (11:14). Peter next refers to the supernatural coming of the Holy Spirit on the audience, apart from all concern for purity regulations and circumcision: 'As I began to speak, the Holy Spirit fell on them, just as on us at the beginning' (11:15).

He also recounts how, at that moment, he remembered the words of Jesus, the undisputed authority accepted by Peter as well as his critics. The event recalled the annunciation of Jesus: 'John baptized with water, but you will be baptized with the Holy Spirit' (11:16). That this announcement was actually given to the Jewish disciples and does not refer to Gentiles, is apparently not an issue. In closing, Peter shares the conclusions which he drew from the vision, from the divine preparation of the encounter and from the coming of the Spirit and which constitute the basis for his disputed behaviour, namely eating with Gentiles (11:3): 'If then God gave the same gift to them as he gave to us when we believed in the Lord Jesus Christ, who was I that I should stand in God's way?'. If God made no distinction, then neither should people distinguish.

The *solution* of conflict comes as Peter's critics accept his explanation for his disputed behaviour (going to Gentiles, staying and eating with them; the legitimacy of the latter was Peter's own interference, not divine prompting): 'And when they heard these things, they fell silent ... and they glorified God, saying, "Then to the Gentiles also God has granted repentance that leads to life"' (11:18). The implication is that Gentiles need not become Jews first before they can participate in God's salvation of Israel. Because God had acted, it was acceptable for Peter to go Gentiles (on divine instruction) and to have fellowship with them. The critics are silenced and the conflict ends in joint glorifying of God.

The solution involved several steps: Peter takes his critics seriously and explains to them in detail the course of the events. His speech in Acts 11 is a shortened summary of the events—the actual speech would have lasted longer than 80 seconds. Inferences from what was *not* said are therefore problematic. As had happened to him before, the critics come to realise the legitimacy of and even the need for Peter's course of action and withdraw their earlier criticism.

In the presentation of Acts, the solution to

the immediate conflict is persistent.³² Acts only now reports on the systematic Gentile mission of Diaspora Jewish Christians from Jerusalem in Antioch (11:19–26), who seem to follow the pattern of the events in Caesarea: they actively go to Gentiles and include them as such in the Christian community (this also happens in Acts 13–14). The next inner-Christian conflict indicates that at least some of the Jewish Christians challenged the generalised conclusion that Gentiles *as Gentiles* had been granted the repentance that leads to life. While Peter's behaviour under these specific circumstances was condoned, no decision was taken regarding the behaviour of *other* Jewish Christians or regarding the procedure concerning *other* Gentiles (must they become proselytes to be part of the community?).

III.3. Acts 15:1–35: The mode of inclusion of Gentiles into the people of God

The conflict in Acts 15 develops in two stages and at two locations. We will first discuss the initial conflict in Antioch (15:1–3) and then its continuation and eventual solution in Jerusalem (15:4–35).

Stage I: Conflict in Antioch without solution

The *occasion* of the third conflict is the legitimacy of the inclusion of Gentiles *as Gentiles* into the people of God—as practised by the nascent Gentile mission of the Hellenists in Antioch and by Antiochene missionaries elsewhere. A number of Christians from Judea (15:24, from Jerusalem?) come to Antioch and teach (ἐδίδασκον, implying a certain claim to authority and systematic approach) the Gentile Christians: 'Unless you are circumcised according to the custom of Moses [i.e., become full proselytes], you cannot be saved [i.e., fully participate in God's salvation for his people]' (15:1).³³ This claim leads to major dissension and debate between these people and Paul and Barnabas, who remained in Antioch after returning from the first Lukan missionary journey (13:1–14:25). As it stands, the critics focus on the Gentile Christians of Antioch. However, their criticism also applies to—or is indirectly aimed at—the practice of Paul and Barnabas. Their practice was known in Antioch ('they declared all that God had done with them, and how he had opened a door of faith to *the Gentiles*', 14:27).

The *contested domain* is the participation of the Gentiles in salvation and the appropriate mode of their inclusion into the people of God. Should they be accepted *as Gentiles* because of their faith in Jesus, or must they also become Jews by being circumcised and becoming obedient to the Law? This issue concerns not only the Gentiles but also has repercussions for Jewish identity and self-understanding: if circumcision or Jewish identity is not necessary for Gentiles, what is its meaning for Jews? Besides the practice of the Diaspora Jewish missionaries from Jerusalem in Antioch the legitimacy of the exploits of Paul and Barnabas on Cyprus and in Asia Minor is also at stake. In addition, through their demand, these Judeans also question Peter's earlier practice in Caesarea (as narrated in Acts 10) and the conclusions drawn from it by the community of Jerusalem in Acts 11:18.

---

32 Wilson, *Luke*, 73, suggests that the Jewish Christians of Acts 11:2 are to be equated with the minority group of Acts 15:5. In this case, their silence in Acts 11:18 would merely be temporal and tactical. Against this identification, Thompson, *One Lord*, 100, rightly refers to 'the near cotext of 10:45 (where a similar group is merely distinguished by their accompaniment with Peter, οἱ ἐκ περιτομῆς πιστοὶ ὅσοι συνῆλθαν τῷ Πέτρῳ) and the response of praise in 11:18b. Thus the effect of the recognition that the Gentiles had received "the same gift" (11:17) from the ascended Lord (11:16; cf. 10:36) was that the "dispute" with the circumcised believers that began in 11:1 was settled. Their objections "ceased" (11:18) "when they heard these things" (ἀκούσαντες δὲ ταῦτα ἡσύχασαν)'.

33 The teaching of Jewish and Gentile Christians is a repeated and significant feature in Acts; see Stenschke, *Luke's Portrait*, 335–344.

The *enabling conditions* on the side of the Judean Christians are significant: what they demand of the Gentiles, namely becoming Jews, is commanded by the Law regarding proselytes (Lev 18:26; 19:33–34; Num 15:14–16; presented by Acts merely as 'the customs of Moses', not as a divine mandate).[34] If these regulations are not followed, membership in God's people is not possible. The Law plays a significant role in Luke-Acts. Especially in Luke's Gospel, obedience to the Law is a sign of piety (however, there are some indications that the Law is relativised there). In view of Paul's personal circumcision of Timothy in Acts 16:3 and of several instances of violence in Acts,[35] it is noteworthy that the Judean Christians *argue* their case—they do not enforce it themselves or incite others to do so.

Paul and Barnabas defend the progressive position by refuting the claim of the Judean Christians. Acts does not indicate how they argued their case, though. Immediately prior to this conflict in Antioch, both men claim divine approval of their mission practice: 'they declared all that *God* had done with them, and how *he* had opened a door of faith to the Gentiles' (14:27). Acts 15:3 notes that the two men's reports regarding the first missionary journey ('describing in detail the conversion of *the Gentiles*') on the way to Jerusalem through both Phoenicia and Samaria brought great joy to all the Christians. In this way, the Judean critics in Antioch appear as an isolated minority. Paul and Barnabas also receive recognition in Jerusalem ('they were welcomed by the church and the apostles and the elders', 15:4) and they report 'all that God had done with them'. In this way, they give glory to God (an indication of their piety) and claim divine approval and prompting for their mission and procedure regarding the Gentiles. These are persuasive enabling factors on their side.

As it proves impossible to de-escalate and solve this conflict in Antioch, and as the parties to this conflict are related to Jerusalem in one way or another (the Judean Christians from Jerusalem?, Barnabas as a Jerusalem emissary to Antioch, and Paul as a former member of the church in Jerusalem), the decision is taken by both parties that the matter should be decided by the apostles and the elders in Jerusalem (15:3). Apparently, they are the acknowledged authority for both parties to this conflict. Both parties seek mediation and an amicable solution to this conflict. Both are concerned about the unity of the church. Paul and Barnabas and some others (perhaps to serve as impartial witnesses) are appointed to present the case in Jerusalem. In view of other conflict narratives in Acts, it is noteworthy that despite major dissension, neither of the parties resort to violent action. Paul and Barnabas do not use their supernatural powers (attested previously; 14:3, 8–10, 19–20) in this conflict (as Paul had done over against a Jewish adversary on Cyprus in Acts 13:6–11).[36]

Stage II: Conflict and Solution in Jerusalem

The occasion for this second round of conflict comprises the warm welcome of the Antiochene delegation in Jerusalem by the church, the apostles and the elders, as well as the reports of 'all that God had done with'

---

34 For a survey see Burns, 'Conversion'.
35 See the instances of forced circumcision of Samaritans in the Hasmonean age.
36 Acts 15:36–41 indicates that not all conflicts between Christians are solved. Paul and Barnabas separate after their sharp disagreement over John Mark. Neither one of them attempts to transfer this case to Jerusalem for decision. For an analysis see Thompson, 'Unity', 539–541. This incident as well as Acts 19:30–31 and 21:1–14 are 'disagreements over how to best serve the same Lord'. They are records of 'varying levels of disagreements among believers. Furthermore, in each instance the dispute appears to remain unresolved in the narrative of Acts. Although Luke indicates a continued common submission to the lordship of Jesus on the part of these believers, he does not portray the unity of the Christian community in an idealised fashion or as uniformity in all matters of personal opinion' (p.541).

Paul and Barnabas (15:4, implying divine affirmation of this mission and its practice). There is no mention of the conflict in Antioch, or of the fact that these Christians had come up to Jerusalem as an official delegation to seek a solution to the conflict in Antioch. This acceptance and the reports move Christian critics in Jerusalem with a Pharisaic background, to action. They make the same demand as the Judean Christians had made in Antioch: 'It is necessary to circumcise them [Gentile Christians] and order them to keep the Law of Moses' (15:5). The Greek word λέγοντες (like 'teaching' in 15:1) does not imply a forceful verbal intervention (see διακρίνω in 11:2; see for comparison the activities of Bar-Jesus/Elymas in Acts 13:8).

The *contested domains* are similar to those found in Antioch. However, they appear intensified: not only must the Gentiles be circumcised in order to obtain salvation (15:1); they must also—explicitly—*keep the Law of Moses* (more than the 'custom of Moses'). Possibly this emphasis or intensification is related to the Pharisaic background of the proponents. The Gentile Christians must become Jews and live accordingly. The Pharisaic Jewish Christians do not demand discussion of these issues, but readily present their conclusions. Their demand concerns the right and authority to determine the conditions of joining the Christian community (the acceptance of Gentiles into the Jewish people of God) and determining and safeguarding its identity. Who has the authority to decide in these matters and how and where should such decisions be taken?

The *enabling conditions* are similar to those of stage I in Antioch. The Pharisaic Jewish Christians have the Old Testament's stipulations regarding proselytes and the ethical guidelines applicable to the people of God on their side, supported by their Pharisaic traditions and practices. They demand that the divinely-ordained Law of Moses be followed. In a day and age when the antiquity of a religious conviction or practice was highly valued, this was a strong argument.[37] In addition, Moses was one of the leading figures of Israel's past.

Paul and Barnabas have the divine affirmation of their ministry on their side. They also have the trust and approval of the Christian community of Antioch. Their reports on the way to Jerusalem brought great joy to all the Christians (15:3). The two men were welcomed by other Christians in Jerusalem (the church, the apostles and the elders). Thus, they are by no means isolated. This rather applies to their opponents.

De-escalation starts with a meeting of the apostles and the elders who take both the visitors from Antioch and the local Pharisaic Jewish Christians seriously (15:6). Acts 15:22 suggests that more people were involved ('Then it seemed good to the apostles and the elders, *with the whole church* ...'). As Paul and Barnabas get to speak as well (15:12), they must have been there and possibly also the Pharisaic Jewish Christians. The public meeting was characterised by much debate. Three contributions to this debate are singled out.

Peter again summarises the events in Caesarea of Acts 10 (already reported in Jerusalem in Acts 11:1–18) with an *emphasis on his own divine appointment and God's actions*: 'God made a choice among you ... God, who knows the heart, bore witness to them, by giving them the Holy Spirit just as he did to us and he made no distinction between us and them, having cleansed their hearts by faith' (15:8–9). To act any different now, that is, to demand full observance of the Law, would mean to put God to the test. In addition, Peter admits that the Jews themselves have not been able to observe the Law anyway. In closing, he affirms that salvation is through the grace of the Lord Jesus, for Jews and Gentiles alike (15:11).

Barnabas and Paul (interestingly, Acts here returns to the initial order of the names) relate once more what signs and wonders God had done through them among the Gentiles. These

---

37 See Pilhofer, *Presbyteron Kreitton*.

signs and wonders indicate divine approval and affirmation of their mission.[38] While some Christians now question its mode, it had full *divine approval*.

James briefly summarises Peter's account ('how God first visited the Gentiles, to take from them a people from his name', 15:14) and argues that these (admittedly surprising) events *agree* with Scripture after all.[39] A new situation requires a new procedure. After a long quotation from the prophet Amos, he presents his conclusion that the Gentiles should not be troubled by the demand to become Jews and to keep the Law of Moses. James suggests some practical stipulation which is aimed at enabling the fellowship of Jewish and Gentile Christians.[40] As the Law of Moses is well-known through regular reading, those who live by it need to be respected.

The *solution* to stage II of this conflict occurs when all—the apostles, the elders and the whole church—agree on James' proposal and see to its proper and efficient communication. The demands of the Pharisaic Jewish Christians are rejected. Their reaction, however, is not noted.

Stage III: Solution of conflict in Antioch

At this point the geographical focus of the narrative returns to *stage I* of the conflict, that is, to *Antioch*. Christians of Jerusalem are to come along with Paul and Barnabas to Antioch. Two named and leading men are appointed to this task.

In addition to the delegation sent to Antioch, the decision is communicated in the form of an official letter (quoted in 15:23–29, 'will tell you the same things by word of mouth', 15:27). The letter clarifies that those who had come down to Antioch from Jerusalem previously, did so without authorisation (15:24). The letter also affirms Paul and Barnabas as 'our beloved Barnabas and Paul' and their authority (15:25). They are recommended as people who have risked their lives for the name of our Lord Jesus Christ (15:26). Judas and Silas are mentioned by name as *official delegates* of the community in Jerusalem (unlike those who had come to Antioch of their own accord). Then the letter communicates the decisions agreed upon (15:28–29). At this juncture, the letter claims that the decision was not only a decision taken by humans, but that it also pleased the Holy Spirit.[41] Thus, it carries divine approval as it agrees with God's prior activities and Scripture (Amos). This is an additional, *transcendent* enabling condition in this conflict.

The delegation is formally commissioned, arrives in Antioch, gathers the congregation together and delivers the letter. All of this happens unlike the previous unauthorised arrival of some Judean Christians who initiated conflict by making demands of their own accord. The letter is read out and well received: 'they rejoiced because of its encouragement' (15:31). Judas and Silas, themselves prophets, encourage and strengthen the Christians in Antioch with great intensity before their return to Jerusalem. The conflict is fully solved and Judas and Silas are sent off 'in peace'. The reaction of the Judean Christians of Acts 15:1 is not noted, though.[42] As was the case before the conflict, Paul and Barnabas remain in Antioch and continue their ministry with many others also.

According to the portrayal of Acts, the

---

38 See Acts 2:22: 'Jesus of Nazareth, a man attested to you by God with mighty works and wonders and signs that God did through him in your midst ...'.
39 For a detailed analysis see Marshall, 'Acts', 589–593.
40 For discussion see Schnabel, Acts, 641–646 and Öhler, *Aposteldekret*.
41 See Wenk, *Community-Forming Power*.
42 It is interesting to note that they are given a voice in the narrative by quoting their demand. However, neither their arguments in the debate with Paul and Barnabas are given, nor their reaction to the decision taken in Jerusalem. The same applies to the Pharisaic Christ-followers in Jerusalem. Who gets to speak and whose voice is being heard/regarded as significant are crucial categories in rhetorical studies, see Watts, 'Voice' and Kritzinger, 'Overcoming'.

solution to this conflict was lasting. The question of whether the Gentiles needed to become Jews and keep the Law of Moses is not raised again in Acts. The decision of the council is explicitly confirmed later in Acts 21:25.[43]

As this study concerns the *portrayal of Acts*, we do not examine the light which Paul's letters may shed on these conflicts. The Jewish Christian opponents mentioned in these letters[44] suggest that not all Jewish Christians agreed with the decision of the council. In view of the fierce controversies in which Paul was involved, critical scholarship with regard to Acts has questioned whether the council actually took place at all, or whether it took place in the way it is presented in Acts.

I. Summary, observations and critical analysis

Summary
The three conflicts which we analysed have different *occasions*: the distribution of material means and the neglect of some in the community; 'going to Gentiles', that is, the behaviour of Jewish Christians and their adherence to Jewish traditions when confronted with Gentiles; and finally, the question under what conditions Gentiles may participate in God's salvation and how they should live accordingly.

The *contested domains* are material resources and/or attention by the apostles, compromises with regard to Jewish identity and life-style, and the conditions for participating in God's salvation and for membership in God's people and the ethical standards which this implies. It is also instructive to see what is not contested in Acts: the identity and significance of Jesus, the community itself as a separate entity over against other groups in early Judaism, experiences of the Holy Spirit, the authority of the Apostles and the inclusion of the Gentiles (while the criteria for inclusion are disputed).

The *enabling conditions* are the direct address of the contested issues (complaining, criticism, including references to tradition and divine revelation (the Law of Moses, the prophet Amos, the words of Jesus), but also experiences and accounts of divine guidance and activity.

The *de-escalations and solutions* of these conflicts are different. These are achieved by tackling the issues, presenting concrete proposals, giving clear instructions, creating new structures (6:1–6); by detailed reporting and explanations of the course of events which led to contested behaviour, including reference to divine guidance and activity and to the words of Jesus (11:1–18); and by generous discussion, reports of the course of events which led a certain position including divine affirmation of contested domains, conclusions based on Scripture and the guidance of the Holy Spirit, proposal of a solution and course of action, and clear and efficient communication (15:1–35). In the course of all three conflicts we notice de-escalation and an eventual solution of conflict. Furthermore, in each case the threatened unity of the community is restored.[45]

Comparison and contrast
In all three conflicts, the causes of conflict/dissension were recognised, taken seriously and attended to, until a solution was reached. While not without conflicts regarding the distribution of material means (a typical contested domain) and the identity and maintenance of its own group identity, the Christ-followers are portrayed as people who manage to resolve conflicts and achieve solutions. In view of the other conflicts we find in Acts, where conflict resolution is difficult or

---

43 The 'conflict' of Acts 21 does not concern Gentiles but Paul's own observance of the Law.
44 On the opponents of Paul see Sumney, *Servants*, and Porter, *Paul*.
45 See Thompson, *One Lord*, 138 notes that in ancient literature, unity often characterises the conquerors while disunity appears with conquered people; see his detailed examination on pp. 105–134.

impossible,[46] it is noteworthy that these inner-Christian conflicts are resolved and the unity of the community is maintained.

With the exception of Antioch in Acts 15:1–2, all inner-community conflicts and the resolution of each involve Christians from Jerusalem and are located in the city.[47] In addition, all of these conflicts occur between *Jewish* Christians (while the occasion in Acts 11 and 15 is the inclusion of Gentiles). The conflict in Antioch is resolved in Jerusalem. The circle of those involved in these conflicts and their resolution widens from the community and the apostles to include the elders, the whole assembly and James.

The implications of the disputed issues are far-reaching (issues of Jewish identity, inclusion of Gentiles as Gentiles into the people of God and the authority to do so and the mode of this inclusion, and all the repercussions which this may have for Jewish identity and the stance of the Christian community in Jerusalem under the critical eyes of other Jews). Still, the course of these conflicts is *mild* in comparison to other conflicts that occur in Acts. There are murmuring, arguing, teaching and eventually 'no small dissension' and 'much debate', but there is no stronger verbal interaction (no pressure is put on the opponents; there is no vilifying, no threats). Those whose position is rejected do not resort to violence (in contrast to the defeated Jewish opponents of the Christian mission, who regularly use violence).

For those involved, some of the contested domains and aspects of these conflicts are *superhuman* (for example, the significance of Jewish identity, and the Law of Moses) and generous reference is made to divine activity and guidance in the course of de-escalation and seeking resolution (11:5–10, 12–15; 15:7, 9, 12).

However, all three conflicts are solved and have to be solved *by humans*. In no case is conflict resolution simply achieved by the Holy Spirit[48] or other divine intervention, of which there is a generous amount elsewhere in Acts. There is no reference to prayer in the context of these conflict solutions. Conflict solution takes time, wisdom and effort.

Only one of these conflicts involves Paul, who dominates the second half of Acts. He is placed in a group with other Christians of Jerusalem, including Barnabas and the Hellenist missionaries who had come to Antioch. According to his letters, Paul was a disputed figure. The Book of Acts, however, portrays Paul as a disputed figure among non-Christian Jews and Gentiles, but not *within* the Christian community (for the significance of this observation, see below).

According to the portrayal of Acts, all three conflict solutions are persistent. Once the issues have been resolved, they do not come up again. The conflict between Judean and Diaspora Jews was resolved (6:1–6); the Christians of Jerusalem accepted Peter's controversial behaviour and the Gentiles as part of the people of God and did not demand that they become Jews and keep the Law of Moses.

It is noteworthy that there is little direct overlap between these inner Jewish-Christian conflicts and the conflicts between the Christian missionaries and the representatives of Diaspora Judaism. There the contested domains are the identity and significance of Jesus of Nazareth and the adherence of Gentile sympathisers, not the mode of the inclusion of Gentiles into the people of God or demands for circumcision, although these must have been disputed issues in this context.

Acts uses reconciliation terminology with regard to Moses' effort of reconciling quarrelling Israelites with each other (7:26). However, these terms are not used regarding the inner-community conflicts. While a

---

46 See Stenschke, 'Interreligious Encounters'; 'Enabling Conditions'; 'Contested Domains Acts 1–5' and 'Contested Domains – Early Christian Mission'.

47 The third conflict arises in Antioch but is transferred for solution to the community in Jerusalem.

48 This is also highlighted by Thompson, 'Unity', 538.

summary statement regarding the increase of the word of God and the multiplication of the number of disciples in Jerusalem appears at the end of the first conflict account (6:7), the earlier statements of unity among the believers are not repeated.[49]

Critical analysis

What are we to make of this picture? *Three issues require attention:*

1) What is the literary function of these accounts of conflict and the solution of each for the Book of Acts? How do they contribute to the purpose of Acts? Obviously, they serve as a contrast: while there was deep division in Israel before, in and through the encounter with Jesus, Israel's Messiah,[50] there is unity among his followers. Although this unity was not without disagreements on several challenging occasions, the community managed to maintain its unity and to stay together. The conflicts which arose were solved. The Christian community is not a quarrelsome lot, but manages its own conflicts and maintains unity in exemplary fashion.[51] Thus, these accounts are an important ingredient in the characterisation of the community of Christ-believers.

However, more is involved in the inclusion of these tales of conflicts and their resolution. They indicate the following:

– The Hellenists / Diaspora Jewish Christ-believers were fully acknowledged by the Jerusalem community.[52] Their leading representatives were elected by the whole community and appointed by the apostles. Therefore, the Hellenistic Jewish Christians who had to leave Jerusalem after the death of Stephen and who started the systematic Gentile mission in Antioch and elsewhere were not isolated figures but people from the midst of the community in Jerusalem and who enjoyed its full approval.

– While not without initial criticism by some, the community of Jerusalem confirmed Peter's activities in Caesarea, that is, 'going to Gentiles' and 'eating/associating with them'. The community confirmed ritual compromises on the side of Jewish Christians evangelising the Gentiles, table fellowship with them and the acceptance of Gentiles as Gentiles into the people of God. All of these had happened when Paul was not yet on the scene. In the narrative, Saul is 'parked' in Tarsus (9:30) and only appears again in Antioch in Acts 11:25–26. He emerges as a Gentile missionary only in Acts 13. Far from being naïve, the community in Jerusalem was fully aware of the implication of the Gentile mission for Jews and Gentiles alike and they agreed on a course of action that was initiated by God himself and affirmed by Scripture and the words of Jesus.

– Despite the demands of some Judean Christians for the Gentiles to be circumcised and to keep the Mosaic Law, the community in Jerusalem stands behind Peter, Hellenistic Jewish Christian missionaries and Paul and his Law-free mission—not without proper reflection,

---

49 This is an *argumentum e silentio*—other characterisations of the early community are not repeated either. The terms for reconciliation in the New Testament hardly appear in Acts. However, they also hardly occur elsewhere in the New Testament with regard to restored relationships between people.
50 See the nuanced analysis by Jervell, 'Divided People'.
51 Thompson, 'Unity', 528, rightly emphasises that Luke 'shows no concern to hide disagreements among believers'.
52 This is also noticed by Thompson, *One Lord*, 95, who writes: 'although Luke opens this account with terms that introduce distinctions among Jews, the account emphasises that in this new community the distinctions do not entail disunity. Thus, throughout ... [Acts 6:1–7] the same term is used for all of those in the community—disciples'.

discussion and resolution of the disputed issues. In doing so, the Christians of Jerusalem recognised divine prompting, understood the developments in view of Scripture, experienced the Spirit's approval and followed it. To have done otherwise in the past and to do otherwise now would mean putting God to the test, as Peter (not Paul!) declares (15:10). Therefore, those who criticise Paul in the author's day appeal in vain to Jerusalem for support.

Surely, a detailed and nuanced portrayal of the inner-Christian conflicts is not the purpose of Acts. At first sight, these accounts appear as mere 'by-products' of Luke's overall apologetic purpose.[53] However, on closer examination it becomes clear that the conflict and solution narratives of Acts make an important contribution to the narrative apology for Paul and his disputed Gentile mission, which is the purpose of Acts.

2) In view of the long history of the church with all its conflicts between Christians and all the frustrations, the question is pressing whether the portrayal of Acts is not all too impressive to be true. Is this portrayal—in part or whole—a construction of the author of Acts for the reasons just outlined? While it surely fits his purposes well, is it historically reliable or at least plausible?[54] Although some summary statements in the early chapters of Acts paint the ideal picture of the Christian community as Israel re-gathered and restored,[55] Acts also reports about the conflicts in their midst (we have focused on three; others could be included, depending on definitions of conflict), even though each of these conflicts is resolved. The Christ-followers are characterised by their unity,[56] despite conflicts.

From the middle of the 19th century onwards, some scholars of early Christianity have argued that all of Acts should be understood not so much as an accurate historical account but rather as an exercise in reconciling the Jewish Christian faction (Jerusalem, Palestinian, Petrine) and the Gentile Christian faction (Antioch, Hellenistic, Pauline) of early

---

53 See Keener, *Acts I*, 435–458.
54 See the excellent discussions in Keener, *Acts I*, 90–220, 320–382 and Thompson, 'Unity', 528.
55 Thompson, 'Unity', refutes the common assumption that 'the presence of the theme of unity in Acts necessarily entails an unrealistic idealisation of the unity of the church' (p.523). He argues that 'the evidence of ancient discussions of unity and the narrative of Acts itself indicate that it is misreading Luke to assume his portrait of the unity of the Christian community is simply unrealistic idealization' (p.523). He demonstrates that 'much discussion of the themes of unity and disunity in ancient literature draws on historical realities' (p.528); discussion on pp. 528–534. Claims that the portrayal of the unity of the church in Acts is not realistic must adequately account for: (1) the prominence of ancient literary discussions of the theme of unity in the context of historical realities; (2) the use of the same language to describe 'united' opponents of the Christian community in the narrative of Acts, and (3) the presence of unresolved disagreements among believers in the narrative of Acts. These 'indicators of reliability' provide supporting evidence that the Lukan interest in the theme of unity is to be read in the context of historical realities rather than unrealistic idealisation (pp.541–542).
56 See the survey in Thompson, 'Unity', 523–524. Thompson notes that disputes within the early Christian community are resolved (p.523). Thompson argues that 'Luke highlights the unity that comes from common submission to the lordship of Jesus rather than uniformity in matters of personal opinion' (p.537).

Christianity.⁵⁷ The conflict narratives are an important ingredient in this endeavour. In its radical form, this hypothesis has come under much criticism and is no longer upheld. However, in a certain way, the author of Acts aims at reconciling Christians with each other by showing the legitimacy of Paul's mission. Those who heard the Gospel from Paul or his many co-workers, can be assured that it is not a minority position (see Luke 1:4),⁵⁸ but has the approval of other followers of Jesus, including his first followers in Jerusalem.

3) Is this portrayal of conflicts and their solution relevant beyond these two questions of interests to New Testament scholarship, and if it is so, in what way?

The steps taken to achieve de-escalation and solution of conflict offer some inspiration for the resolution of present-day conflicts between Christians and also between other people. This is all the more pertinent within the church, were these accounts as part of canonical scripture are read regularly and cherished. In one way or another, they shape the self-understanding of the community and of its ideals. Where and when they are not read and reflected upon, something important is missing.

While the original occasions of conflict in Acts change over time and in different contexts, some of the *contested domains* of the past remain contested issues: the distribution of material resources, attention by leaders given to different groups and issues of equality among different groups of believers; the identity of the own group, its privileges and duties, and how it should relate to others (making contact and associating with 'outsiders'); the way in which people deal with their traditions and authoritative scriptures amidst changing circumstances; and the conditions under which others are to be included into the in-group.⁵⁹

What about the *enabling conditions*, the prerequisites for a conflict to run its course? In the conflicts of Acts, there is exemplary verbal interaction (raising issues, discussion, drawing conclusions, amicable agreement and proper communication). Obviously, some aspects of these accounts are less natural today and they have also been abused: the recourse to established authority (tradition, Scripture) has become ambiguous in some contexts; God's working in history is no longer as obvious, fresh or easy to be recognised.

It is interesting to observe that in our accounts there is no use of verbal violence (which has come to the fore in recent discussions of religious conflict—see Mayer) or physical violence (still the emphasis of much research on religious conflict). The portrayals of the parties to these conflicts whose position is eventually rejected are friendly, not vilifying. Even Peter, as the leader of the apostolic band and repeatedly divinely affirmed, can be questioned and called to account by rank-and-file Christians.

The steps taken in the de-escalation and resolution of these conflicts are timeless: time is granted to explain; people listen to each other and weigh arguments;

---

57 For a survey see Gasque, History, 21–135; Harris, *Tübingen School*, and Thompson, *One Lord*, 3–4. For the claim of Acts as idealising the unity of the church unrelated to historical reality see the survey by Thompson, 'Unity', 525–526. Thompson notes that 'the idealisation is primarily said to be (1) an attempted cover up for deep division; (2) a nostalgic (and uninformed) look back to the past; or (3) a creative (and unrealistic) portrait of a Golden Age beginning' (p.525).
58 For the audience of Acts see Thompson, *One Lord*, 10–13.
59 These issues are within the range of insights and theories of the social sciences (social identity theory, social psychology, etc.).

there is room for ample discussion without verbal or physical violence (in marked contrast to the other conflicts of Acts). People receive, recognise and respond to divine affirmation and guidance (where applicable); there is recourse to Scripture for guidance and the readiness to act, even though it involves risk.

From our perspective it may be surprising that other than possible or probable contributions to the 'much debate' mentioned in Acts 15:7, Acts does not give the Pharisaic Christians of Jerusalem an opportunity to present their case in detail or to refute the position of Peter, Barnabas and Paul or James (voice vs voicelessness). For the author of Acts, who clearly privileges the case he wants to present, their position cannot be refuted.

The conflict of Acts 6:1–6 only occurs because the number of the disciples (originally 120) who had come with Jesus from Galilee increased drastically and included people from different backgrounds (the Hellenists). The occasions of the conflicts of Acts 10 and 15 were encounters of Jewish Christians with Gentiles,[60] the mode of their inclusion into the community and the implications of this inclusion for Jewish believers. The conflict accounts of Acts remind us that communities whose horizons are broadened, which encounter new situations and people, and whose traditions and identity are challenged and modified are likely to experience conflict. The question is *whether* they are willing and able to deal with such conflicts and *how* they do so. The events which generated these conflicts and their solution can broaden theological horizons. In our case, they brought new people (who played a significant role later on) into leadership positions and deepened the understanding of God's intentions and of the identity of the community and its role.

The Book of Acts presents a Christian community that is not harmonious and ideal, but had its significant dissensions and conflicts. It allows for dissension (murmuring) and open discussion (even criticism) – a community in which leaders can be questioned and are held to account; a community where those who disagree can take the initiative and also have a voice. It is all too evident that the church has not always followed this pattern. The fact that the community managed to resolve these conflicts (and how it went about it), is one of the abiding legacies of the portrayal of the early Christian community in Acts.

---

60 For a survey see Stenschke, 'Interreligious Encounters'.

List of References

Burns, Joshua E.   'Conversion and Proselytism', in J. J. Collins, D. C. Harlow (eds.), *The Eerdmans Dictionary of Early Judaism* (Grand Rapids: Eerdmans, 2010), 484–86.

Cullmann, Oscar   'Dissensions Within the Early Church', *USQR* 22 (1967) 83–92.

Frey, Jörg, Claire K. Rothschild, & Jens Schröter (eds.) *Die Apostelgeschichte im Kontext antiker und frühchristlicher Historiographie* (BZNW 162; Berlin, New York: De Gruyter, 2009).

Gasque, W. Ward   *A History of the Interpretation of the Acts of the Apostles* (Peabody; Hendrickson, ²1989).

Goulder, Michael   *St. Paul versus St. Peter: A Tale of Two Missions* (Louisville: Westminster John Knox, 1995).

Gudehus, Christian, Michaela Christ (eds.)   *Gewalt: Ein interdisziplinäres Handbuch* (Stuttgart, Weimar: J. B. Metzler, 2013).

Haacker, Klaus   *Die Apostelgeschichte* (ThKNT 5; Stuttgart: Kohlhammer, 2019).

Harris, Horton   *The Tübingen School* (Oxford: Clarendon, 1975).

Hume, David A.   *The Early Christian Community: A Narrative Analysis of Acts 2:41–47 and 4:32–35* (WUNT II.298; Tübingen: Mohr Siebeck, 2011).

Jennings, W. J.   *Acts* (TCB; Louisville: Westminster John Knox, 2017).

Jervell, Jacob   'The Divided People of God: The Restoration of Israel and Salvation for the Gentiles', in J. Jervell, *Luke and the People of God: A New Look at Luke-Acts* (Minneapolis: Augsburg, 1972), 41–74.

Juergensmeyer, Mark, Margo Kitts, Michael Jerryson (eds.)   *The Oxford Handbook of Religion and Violence* (Oxford: Oxford University Press, 2013).

Keener, Craig S.   *Acts: An Exegetical Commentary* Vol. I: *Introduction and 1:1–2:47* (Grand Rapids: Baker, 2012).

Keener, Craig S.   *Acts: An Exegetical Commentary* Vol. II: *3:1–14:28* (Grand Rapids: Baker, 2013).

Keener, Craig S.   *Acts: An Exegetical Commentary* Vol. III: *15:1–23:35* (Grand Rapids: Baker, 2014).

Kritzinger, Johannes   'Overcoming Theological Voicelessness in the New Millennium', *Missionalia* 40 (2012), 233–50.

Marshall, I. Howard   'Acts', in G. K. Beale and D. A. Carson (eds.), *Commentary on the New Testament use of the Old Testament* (Nottingham: IVP, 2007), 513–606.

Mayer, Wendy   'Religious Conflict: Definitions, Problems and Theoretical Approaches', in W. Mayer, B. Neil (eds.), *Religious Conflict from Early Christianity to the Rise of Islam* (AKG 121; Berlin, Boston: De Gruyter, 2013), 1–19.

Öhler, Markus (ed.)	*Aposteldekret und antikes Vereinswesen: Gemeinschaft und ihre Ordnung* (WUNT 280; Tübingen: Mohr Siebeck, 2011).
Peterson, David G.	*The Acts of the Apostles* (PNTC; Grand Rapids: Eerdmans, 2009).
Pilhofer, Peter	Presbyteron Kreitton: *Der Altersbeweis der jüdischen und christlichen Apologeten und seine Vorgeschichte* (WUNT II.39; Tübingen: Mohr Siebeck, 1990).
Porter, Stanley E. (ed.)	*Paul and His Opponents*, Pauline Studies 2 (Leiden: Brill, 2005).
Rakotoharintsifa, Andrianjatovo	'Luke and the Internal Divisions in the Early Church', in C. M. Tuckett (ed.), *Luke's Literary Achievement: Collected Essays* (LNTS 116; Sheffield: Sheffield Academic Press, 1995), 165–77.
Roloff, Jürgen	'Konflikte und Konfliktlösungen nach der Apostelgeschichte', in C. Bussmann, W. Radl (eds.), *Der Treue Gottes trauen: Beiträge zum Werk des Lukas* (Freiburg, Basel, Wien: Herder, 1991), 111–25.
Schnabel, Eckhard J.	*Acts* (ZECNT; Grand Rapids: Zondervan, 2012).
Stenschke, Christoph	*Luke's Portrait of Gentiles Prior to Their Coming to Faith* (WUNT II.108; Tübingen: Mohr Siebeck, 1999).
Stenschke, Christoph	'"... sandten die Apostel zu ihnen Petrus und Johannes" (Apg 8,10): Überörtliche Verbindungen der urchristlichen Gemeinden in der Darstellung der Apostelgeschichte des Lukas', *EThL* 87 (2011), 433–53.
Stenschke, Christoph	'Interreligious Encounters in the Book of Acts', in H. Hagelia, M. Zehnder (eds.), *Interreligious Relations: Biblical Perspectives: Proceedings from the Second Norwegian Summer Academy of Biblical Studies (NSABS)* (T & T Clark Biblical Studies; London, Oxford, New York: Bloomsbury T & T Clark, 2017), 135–79.
Stenschke, Christoph	'"Enabling Conditions" in the Conflicts of Acts 1–8:3', *Journal of Early Christian History* 7, 2017, 54–86.
Stenschke, Christoph	'"Contested Domains" in Religious Conflict: A Case Study of Acts 1–5', *Asian Horizons: Dharmaram Journal of Theology* 11 (2017), 504–20.
Stenschke, Christoph	'"Contested Domains" in the Conflicts Between the Early Christian Mission and Diaspora Judaism According to the Book of Acts', in W. Mayer, C. de Wet (eds.), *Reconceiving Religious Conflict: New Views From the Formative Centuries of Christianity* (Routledge Studies in the Early Christian World; London: Routledge, 2018), 139–81.
Sumney, Jerry L.	*"Servants of Satan", "False Brothers" and Other Opponents of Paul* (JSNT.S 188; Sheffield: Sheffield Academic Press, 1999).
Thompson, Alan J.	'Unity in Acts: Idealization or Reality?"' *JETS* 51 (2008), 523–42.
Thompson, Alan J.	*One Lord, one People: The Unity of the Church in Acts in Its Literary Setting* (LNTS 359; London: Bloomsbury T. & T Clark, 2012).

Watts, Eric King	'Voice and Voicelessness in Rhetorical Studies', *Quarterly Journal of Speech* 87 (2001), 179–96.
Wenk, Matthias	*Community-Forming Power: The Socio-Ethical Role of the Spirit in Luke-Acts* (JPTSS 19; Sheffield: Sheffield Academic Press, 2000).
Wilson, Stephen G.	*Luke and the Law* (SNTSMS 50; Cambridge: Cambridge University Press, 1983).
Yarbrough, Robert W.	'Forgiveness and Reconciliation', in T. D. Alexander, B. S. Rosner (eds.), *New Dictionary of Biblical Theology* (Leicester: IVP, 2000), 498–503.
Zugmann, Michael	*"Hellenisten" in der Apostelgeschichte: Historische und exegetische Untersuchungen zu Apg 6,1; 9,29, 11,20* (WUNT II.264; Tübingen: Mohr Siebeck, 2009).

Book reviews

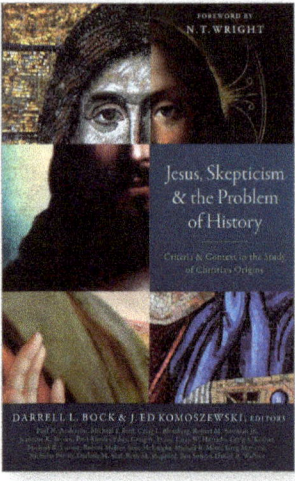

Darrell L. Bock, *Jesus, Skepticism & the Problem of History*
(HarperCollins Religious - US, 2019)

A book report and some core issues[1]

Jesus, Skepticism & The Problem of History, edited by Ed Komoszewski and myself with a Foreword by Tom Wright (Zondervan, 2019) is a book on the current state of Historical Jesus study from an evangelical perspective. Our core goal was to ask questions about the state of such studies, especially in light of recent work on *Jesus, Criteria and the Demise of Authenticity*, ed. by Chris Keith and Anthony Le Donne. This work mostly challenged the role of the criteria as flawed, a view that goes back to critiques decades ago by Morna Hooker. It raised a question about whether historical Jesus study was becoming a spent force with nowhere to go. Keith and Le Donne still expressed a hope of engaging such questions but our volume wondered if the skepticism about the criteria, though fair to express as a check on its use, had taken one too many steps. The questions in our minds remained: where did that leave us, what methods should we pursue and were the criteria so problematic as to be useless?

Our book was comprised of 14 essays plus three responses and the already noted foreword. We chose not to give any introduction or responses to the responders to let the dialogue simply take place, since the raising of issues was a primary goal of the volume. There were 18 essayists (four essays had a pair of authors). Three women were among them (in two single pieces and one in a paired essay). I will simply overview the essays to present the direction of the book.

A chapter by Ed Komozewski and Robert Bowman "The Historical Jesus and the Biblical Church: Why the Quest Matters" overviewed the issues tied to Historical Jesus study. It reviewed the three quests, the many Jesuses those quests have produced and observed that both historical and philosophical questions were bound up in such work. The issue of miracles offered a particular challenge within this material, something Mike' Licona's later piece also noted. To what extent was the historical Jesus, the real Jesus? Komoszewski and Bowman argue there is a tighter relationship than many allow. The church seeks to know him in both those forms.

Craig Blomberg and Darlene Seal wrote about "The Historical Jesus in Recent Evangelical Scholarship." Noting the impact of work by Sanders, Crossan, Wright, and Dunn from 1985 to 2003. This period was the last heyday for such study, even getting more public attention for the conversation these works engendered. They went on to note a wider range of views from mythicists

---

[1] This report was initially delivered at the Centre for Gospels and Acts Research Quarterly Meeting on 14 July 2020. I am grateful for the feedback given on that occasion.

like Robert Price to evangelical skeptics about historical Jesus work like David Farnell. Blomberg and Seal asked where evangelicals fit in the mix with three general candidates present: eschatological prophet, social change agent and marginalized Jewish Messiah. They argued the messianic claimant category has the most potential to be of help. The backdrops of Jewish context, issues tied to memory and orality and working back from effects to cause are all in play in significant ways as historical Jesus work gets done. They listed a plethora of evangelicals whose work fell in this area: Craig Evans, Michael Bird, Graham Twelftree, Klyne Snodgrass, Michael Licona, Craig Keener, and myself were named explicitly. Focus was given to *Key Events in the Life of the Historical Jesus*, an edited work by myself and Robert Webb for the IBR Historical Jesus group, that involved over a half dozen scholars, originally published in WUNT in 2009. Such study was important from a historical perspective as it took on twelve core events arguing on historical-critical grounds for the essential authenticity of these specific accounts, while being able to highlight a consistency about who Jesus was, as well as what was distinctive in Jesus's teaching. One of the key means of doing this work did involve appeals to the criteria. They note that Dagmar Winter, a contributor to the Keith and Le Donne volume, still made use of criteria, including the plausibility criteria proposed by Theissen and Merz. One suggestion made is that the Gospel of John can come into more play than it has in past historical Jesus work, a point made in a longer essay by Paul Anderson that appealed for a fourth quest by outlining in detail how that Gospel has been handled (or better often ignored) in historical Jesus work up until recently. Anderson made the case for how to reconnect John to the larger discussion.

Going a different direction was Michael Metts' "Neglected Discontinuity between Early Form Criticism and the New Quest with Reference to the Last Supper". He challenged how much the Keith and Le Donne volume blamed links to Form Criticism for the flaws in the criteria. Here we have not only a look back on how historical Jesus study developed but also the injection of a specific text to look at how that discussion applied in a particular case. The discontinuity between early Form Criticism and the New Questers argued that the New Quest did not simply inherit more skeptical early Form Critical approaches as the Keith Le Donne study claimed, but was a move in a more accepting direction of the development in the tradition and its occasional links back to Jesus. This essay was designed to qualify some of what Chris Keith argued in the *Demise* volume. Käsemann was a long step away from the thorough skepticism of Bultmann because this student of Bultmann saw some strands of continuity between Jesus and the theology of the early church. A defense of the criterion of dissimilarity, not as a defining criterion but as useful in limited ways, concluded that essay.

Dan Wallace's "Textual Criticism and the Criterion of Embarrassment" argued on the basis of several specific textual units that embarrassment caused copyists to alter the text. This was a backhanded way to show that embarrassment was still at work after the Gospels were produced and to show the validity of that criterion in looking at the texts themselves.

"Collective Memory and the Reliability of the Gospel Traditions" was Robert McIver's update of his earlier work, *Memory, Jesus and the Synoptic Gospels* (2012)—a work he produced on Sabbatical while in Tübingen where I happened to be his neighbor for a time in the Dozentenwohnheim. Here McIver concentrated on the fact that corporate or collective memory does not work in the same way as individual memory, which is what most memory studies invoked for Jesus studies investigated. This question looks at the important issue of how the tradition developed and was recalled. He argued that even over time collective memory has staying power. Even when there are issues of differing details, it often did have connections to real events.

Paul Eddy also dealt with orality issues in "The Historicity of Early Jesus Tradition: Reflections of the 'Reliability Wars'". He discussed what he calls the pessimistic and optimistic trajectories that such discussion generates. Here we think of Rudolf Bultmann and Werner Kelber (pessimistic) versus Ken Bailey and Richard Bauckham (optimistic). Eddy warned about generalizations concerning the oral process that did not look at the kind of material being passed on. Orality concerns were impacted by genre. Narrative genres about real events were passed on with more care than ones seen as fictional from the start. The issue of passing on material within the memory of living participants was not the same as later efforts to pass material on. The impulse in passing on tradition in many communities was a conserving one. Narrative plot lines allowed for development of longer narratives in oral preservation. Custodians of the tradition often exist early on and kept it from roaming too far. Tradition and authoritative teachers are a key here.

> **Custodians of the tradition ... kept it from roaming too far.**

Jeannine Brown discussed "Reconstructing the Historical Pharisees: Does Matthew's Gospel have Anything to Contribute?". Purity issues, eating habits, social roles and political aims came in for attention here, as did a focus on Matthew 23. The way the Pharisees were described involved historically plausible contours with cultural coherence. Ideas that this only reflected Matthew's setting are overdrawn.

Beth Shepherd's "Alternate History and the Sermon on the Mount: New Trajectories for Research" examined how cultural history and alternate history might help us sort through issues in a passage. She warned about the danger of bypassing singularly attested material that could be relevant, with another tip of the hat to John's Gospel. She argued for being sure the Greco-Roman cultural context was placed alongside Jewish sources in a culture that was so mixed with influences. Alternate history involves counterfactual, creative work immersed in first century cultural contexts. Bruce Longenecker's work with Paul in *Letters to Pergamum* and Gerd Theissen's *The Shadow of the Galilean* are cited as examples, both of which explore the culture through recreating fuller accounts of context in fictitious ways that have a verisimilitude with ancient reality. She considered the possibility that Jesus's address on the Mount might have included a theater setting.

My essay "A Test Case: Jesus' Remarks before the Sanhedrin: Blasphemy or Hope of Exaltation" revisited a topic I have spent over two decades on. It was designed to be a sample study of how to look at a particular text. Using two key criteria (multiple attestation and rejection and execution) as well as working very hard on the cultural backdrop of blasphemy and exaltation, it argued for historical plausibility. One can have some confidence that what we are told about this scene largely reflected what took place. I even worked to make a case for the sayings in the material. Multiple attestation helped us with a title like Son of Man being a part of Jesus's self-expression. The use of Ps. 110:1 showed evidence of being characteristic of Jesus. A circumspect appeal to the criteria can help us in certain texts.

I have already noted the work of Paul Anderson. He looks at the "John, Jesus and History Project and a Fourth Quest for Jesus". We gave him more space to develop this line of study because of the lack of space John's Gospel normally receives in historical Jesus studies. Anderson gave a full historical overview and apologetic for why John needs to be taken more seriously and gave a solid rationale for a fourth quest that consciously includes his Gospel.

Craig Evans and Greg Monette presented "Jesus' Burial: Archaeology, Authenticity and History". They defended yet another key event, the burial of Jesus, as highly probable and did so through two criteria: multiple attestation and embarrassment. For example, naming Joseph of Arimathea would be quite embarrassing in the living memory of some if the connection had been fabricated. The flight of the disciples on Jesus's arrest was another such detail. The way Jesus was buried fit Roman custom for one executed. A convicted and executed felon could not be laid in a family tomb. This was a dishonor that was to remain for the one who opposed the state, one convicted of a crime.

In "Jesus's Resurrection, Realism and the Role of the Criteria of Authenticity", Michael Licona returned to a favorite topic of his, the Resurrection. Three issues drove his conversation: the role of miracles and whether history can deal with them; the general ability of historians to learn the past; and whether criteria can help us in the quest. He directly challenged an approach called "methodological naturalism" that says history simply was not capable of going into the miraculous. He argued if the best explanation of an event versus other hypotheses included a miraculous element, then it was appropriate to consider it and conclude so. He contended that we can get to the core of what the past was about. We can find what is "true enough" and the criteria can be of help here. Multiple attestation, the early nature of resurrection reports, and the embarrassing features to passing details point to this event's credibility. For example, if we take Gethsemane seriously, Jesus did not go to his death as a bold martyr. Although Licona does not mention it, one could add the role of women in the empty tomb accounts as another example, since a controversial concept initially is defended by witnesses who culturally did not count as witnesses. A created story was unlikely to have started here.

These essays complete the look at the Gospels. Two more essays work with parallel material in Acts. Michael Bird and Ben Sutton looked at "Social Memory in Acts". Appreciating how orality works was a point in this essay.

There is an economy in passing things on that can work effectively as tradition develops. Craig Keener closed out with "Acts: History or Fiction?". He looked at events and local color in Acts and compared them to external evidence to argue against a fictitious Acts, which in turn reflected on Luke and his Gospel for its handling of events. We can approach Luke's history with "great confidence".

This survey reflected the core emphases in our volume. I commend the responses, which strike me as fair in contributing to the give and take the volume is designed to engender. They argued that perhaps the distance between the Keith and Le Donne volume and ours was not as great as the choice of making it a foil might suggest. We think we have shown the limited value of some of the criteria, the importance of careful cultural work, and the nature of the orality process in a corporate context, all of which should minimize the skepticism common in many treatments of the Gospels. In sum, evangelical historical Jesus study is alive and well and contributes to the larger discussion in the field. It serves the church and all by pointing to potential core historical reality that is tied to Jesus as portrayed in the Gospels.

> **We can get to the core of what the past was about.**

Some issues that remain

In this concluding section I make a few, very brief notes about some of the core issues that are a part of historical Jesus study even before one looks at specific texts. The list is not exhaustive by any means, but it does reflect the range of issues one has to be aware of even to walk into such study. Anyone who works in the field will not be surprised by this limited list, but those just beginning may find the enumeration helpful. There is more to examining Gospel texts for their historical content, than just the texts themselves.

Orality: how does it work?

As our book showed, there is much conversation about the period between the events and their recording in the Gospels. This "event to written recording" gap of several decades raises all kinds of questions about how traditions developed in a primarily oral culture. When a new community's identity is at stake that was tied to a person and events, how did that work? How is corporate memory like or unlike individual memory? Does potential oversight of such tradition impact its quality? Does the fact many of these events were repeatedly recited play a role in how they were passed on and recalled? Does that fact distort studies that look at how events were recalled by individuals with the only time gap in mind being between the event and the time of study? Does the fact that ancient culture was primarily oral mean they were better at it than we are, given how many other means we have to recall things? Where are our best analogies for such study, in folklore, ancient heroic accounts, rabbinic models or elsewhere?

Authenticity and criteria

What is the role and value of criteria? Given their acknowledged flaws, are they usable? If one abandons them, what does that leave us with to try and adjudicate the quality of the recorded events? Are these kinds of standards like those used outside of Gospel literature as we assess other ancient texts? Is the approach in dealing with events the same as those for sayings? How can one have this discussion about the accounts being true with someone who does not trust Scripture as even being generally reliable if there is lacking some type of standard to appeal to, in order to weigh what is seen? In other words, on what basis does one deal with a skepticism that may say you have to prove the value of the text to me?

Epistemology and its subset on historiography

How much history is good enough for these conversations? Is history one dimensional, being rooted for authenticity only in what was at the original time or does the framing of history by a wider scope of events allow for a legitimate refracting of historical impact that is nevertheless historical and authentic? Is it all or nothing? Does history have layers when it comes to temporal perspectives where what may have been implicit emerges to be explicit over time so that a link back does still exist? How do we deal with variations in details versus the thrust of the tradition about who Jesus was, especially when those themes appear to be more coherent and consistent? Should we expect sources rooted to some degree in people who were with Jesus to get the core baseline of his self-understanding correct? If the tradition feeding the Gospels is not a matter only of discussing the authors but of their traditional roots, then does there not exist a potential case for a response to more skeptical takes on those texts? What were the ancient expectations when it came to writing history? Did ancient know the difference between reaching back to understand an event and fabrication of events? Did they care? Was there one such universal standard or did such expectations vary making generalizations about ancient history writing a challenge in itself? Are Bible believers simply misguided "positivists"?

Issue of macro-micro role of narrative and compositional methods (how critics divide and conquer):

Is biblical evidence so carved up by critics that issues tied to historicity are undercut by delinking the narrative whole and thrust of a Gospel argument? Here debates about authenticity and the Son of Man come to mind. Only by separating what was presented as linked can one even begin to make a credible argument against such sayings going back to Jesus on whose lips that specific virtually always appears. Work like that of Tom Wright and others have come to stress looking at the whole macro argument for Gospel material versus cutting it up into little pieces and as a result risk severing what may have been linked. *Key Events* was an attempt to honor both the micro and macro levels, while contending that coherence can still be the result while applying standards most historical Jesus scholars use.

How does theology shape our method?

Clearly theology and worldview impact how we evaluate what we see. A naturalist approach is automatically challenged by the very way the Gospel accounts are framed by miracles and claims of God's activity and presence. Those who have a high regard for Scripture are usually slow to see issues and problems. Claims of neutrality with regard to the text are probably regularly overblown. But bias need not mean an inability to be reflective and critical about what is in the text or the issues tied to engaging it. When skepticism meets those of faith, then a question becomes, how do we even try to have this conversation given the interpreters' different starting points?

Limits of historical method: How far can history take us really?

We all know we have limited remains and artifacts from a cultural context far removed from us while dealing with all these methodological challenges (and my list has been selective!). So how far can history really take us? I would suggest we have no choice but to try but to do so being self-aware and self-critical about how we approach these issues. There is so much at stake in how we see the human condition that these culturally significant texts raise, and the history of the influence of Jesus is undeniable. So the conversation continues with all these layers of questions being a part of how we must proceed, even before we get to the texts themselves.

Darrell L. Bock
Dallas Theological Seminary

BOOK REVIEWS

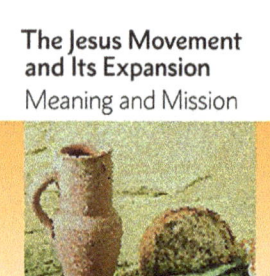

Seán Freyne, *The Jesus Movement and Its Expansion: Meaning and Mission* (Grand Rapids & Cambridge, UK: Eerdmans, 2014)

Seán Freyne (1935–2013) was professor emeritus of theology at Trinity College in Dublin and a well-known specialist on ancient Galilee as the place of the ministry of Jesus. The current volume had its origin in the Schafer lectures, delivered in Yale in 2010 and it focuses on the rise and expansion of early Christianity within the ambience of the Greco-Roman world.

In the introduction (pp.1–10), Freyne writes with regard to his position and presuppositions:

> It is my belief that the emphasis on Galilee in recent writing on the historical Jesus, while important in giving a specific location for the public ministry, is in danger of distorting the picture, by appearing to set up an opposition between Galilee and Jerusalem. Clearly there were differences, partly those that pertain to the relationship of a religious capital with its more remote hinterland, and partly because of the economic and social differences to the point of speaking about Galilean Judaism in opposition to its Judean counterpart, as though they were hostile neighbours, flies in the face of what we know about the situation from literary, historical, and archaeological sources (pp.1–2).

The aim is to provide an informed view of Jesus through a better understanding of his Jewish up-bringing and practice as well as the possible influence of Greco-Roman values and lifestyles on him and his followers (p.2). For this quest, Freyne also emphasises the importance of the archaeological evidence discovered in the past four decades in various regions and on various sites (pp.2–3). This evidence adds to our understanding of the social conditions and cultural affiliations of the inhabitants of Hellenistic and Roman Judea. Freyne's astute survey of such discoveries is worth quoting in full:

> Ceramic objects, such as pots, pans, and jugs for water and wine tell us about cooking and dietary practices. Vine and olive installations are pointers to the ways in which local produce was harvested and prepared for both domestic and religious use as well as for export. Boats, harbours and other fishing objects are indicators of the importance of the fish industry in the lake region. Building techniques, imported artefacts, decorative aspects such as stuccoed walls and mosaic ornamentation help to distinguish between the rich and powerful and the poor and the oppressed. Milestones and remains of ancient roads tell us about the movements of people for trading and other engagements, as well as the routes taken by ancient armies and pilgrims alike. Coins serve to illustrate the propaganda slogans and images of the ruling elites, as well as provide some indications of the levels of trade and commerce that took place. Tombs tell their own story of regional burial customs and different beliefs about the afterlife. Dedicatory inscriptions can provide important information about the purpose

of various public buildings and the particular deities that were worshipped. Stepped pools and public buildings with benches suggest respect for Jewish rituals and religious gatherings away from Jerusalem and the temple. Regional surveys can provide information about demographic changes at different periods. ... the list is endless, but constantly fascinating for the ancient historian and the modern traveller alike (pp.2–3).

Chapters one to three offer a comprehensive discussion of the *matrix* of Greco-Roman Judea. 'Matrix' (rather than background) 'implies a living, dynamic environment that is constantly interacting with the various levels of human life and activity that is taking place' (p.3). This environment 'assists us in envisaging and being attentive to a complex set of relationships that are operative and at play as the various actors go about their daily chores' (p.3).

Chapter one, 'Galilee of the Gentiles?' (pp.13–51), summarises the process and effect of Hellenisation on all aspects of life in Judea since Alexander the Great (Hellenistic reform and Judean resistance, Judeans in Galilee, survey of the Greek cities encircling Galilee and their influence on the situation there). Freyne concludes that Jews in both Galilee and Jerusalem did not completely turn their back on the Greek world. 'Rather, many availed themselves of the opportunities that were on offer within the larger context while resisting any easy assimilation to that culture, especially its religion' (p.47).

Chapter two examines the history of 'The Roman Presence' in Judea from the middle of the first century B.C.E. up to the two revolts against Rome in 66–70 and 132–135 C.E. (pp.52–89; Herod the Great and his relation to Imperial ideology, the architecture, coinage, and cult of Antipas and Philip, developments toward the first Jewish revolt and its immediate aftermath, the fate and positions of the Judean Jesus-followers and the fall of Jerusalem, closing with a survey of Rome and Judea between the revolts, 70–135 C.E.).

Chapter three offers an up-to-date survey of Judean economy and society from the Hellenistic to the Roman period (pp.90–132). The aim is to gain a better understanding of the situation that prevailed for ordinary people when Jesus began his public ministry in Galilee. Freyne draws on the results of archaeological explorations for documenting these developments and producing an accurate profile of conditions in Jerusalem and Galilee in particular. Rather than allowing one of the several recent models to dictate the resultant picture, Freyne does not rely on any one model but combines both a deductive approach based on actual evidence with an inductive application of various theoretical scenarios, in the hope of arriving at the best fit between evidence and social theory in our present state of knowledge (p.6).

> **Jews in both Galilee and Jerusalem did not completely turn their back on the Greek world.**

Regarding the first three chapters, Freyne concludes:

> (1) that the epithet 'Galilee of the Gentiles' is not an appropriate description of the region's ethos from the second Century B.C.E. onward, (2) that there are unmistakable signs of continued Jewish practice and observance throughout the region, despite the 'intrusion' of the Herodians, and (3) that, while there is no trace of economic or social decline in some of the larger villages, nevertheless the likelihood is that social differentiation increased among the peasantry during the reign of Antipas (p.132).

Chapter four, central in the book; is devoted to the actual *ministry* of the historical Jesus, despite all the attendant obstacles that our sources impose on such an enterprise. Freyne notes that his approach here is not substantially different from that of his early study *Jesus, a*

Jewish Galilean: New Reading of the Jesus Story (p.6). That is, Freyne emphasises:

> Jesus' indebtedness to his own Judean and Israelite heritage, especially that of the Sabbath and Jubilee years, and the importance of the landscape in shaping his responses to the situations he encountered. Josephus' account of Jesus' ministry of word and work in his teaching and healing ministry provides the framework for examining his activity in both these spheres and evaluating its significance. The choice of the Twelve as his permanent retinue places his whole ministry under the banner of Israelite/Judean restoration hopes, and his excursions to what may have been deemed as Gentile territory can also be explained within the framework of what may be called 'the geography of restoration'. This was based on the information about the ideal boundaries for the land as these continued to be recalled in various circles over the centuries (pp.6–7).

The chapter closes with an examination of Jesus' understanding of the future, including the admission of Gentiles and the circumstances of his death by crucifixion.

Chapters five to eight focus on the *mission* and expansion of the Jesus movement in Judea and beyond during the first hundred years of its development. *Chapter 5* focuses on the significance of the resurrection, the importance of Jerusalem as centre of the early church, the portrayal of this community in Acts, the distinction between the Hebrews and the Hellenists and their understanding of the mission to the Gentiles. *Chapter six* aims at discovering traces of the Jesus-followers in Galilee and its environs, as seen through the lens of the various sayings sources that are available, especially the Q source, the Gospel of Thomas and the Didache. *Chapter seven* reads in particular Mark and Matthew against the backdrop of the worsening political situation in Judea prior to the war in 66–70 C.E. and its immediate aftermath. In closing, *chapter eight* traces the transition from the 'New Testament' period to later generations as the Christian movement began to acquire a much higher profile, but also greater diversity, in the second century. The discussion includes issues of orthodoxy and heresy, the ongoing relationship with the Jewish world, and the need to negotiate the case for being a *religio licita*, not a *nova superstitio*, within the Roman world.

There are a number of questionable issues in chapters five to eight (dating of the Gospels, presupposition of Q, the Gospels as windows into later developments …); however, Freyne's emphases in chapter four deserve full attention and careful appraisal. All readers of the Gospels will appreciate Freyne's fine description and analysis of the 'matrix' in the first chapters which summarise Freyne's work on Galilee, Jesus and the Gospels over many years; for a similar approach see M. Hengel & A. M. Schwemer, *Jesus and Judaism* (Baylor – Mohr Siebeck Studies in Early Christianity; Tübingen: Mohr Siebeck, 2019).

While the term Judea is in itself ambiguous (reference to Jerusalem and its surroundings or wider Judea), the term *Palestine* (mostly used by Freyne) is also problematic. Although it might serve as an established and convenient geographical designation, its origin (coined by the Roman victors after 135 C.E. as an ideological programme to eradicate Jewish identity from the area) and use are anachronistic for the first century. It should not be used in historical studies.

Christoph Stenschke
Biblisch-Theologische Akademie Wiedenest
and Department of Biblical and Ancient Studies
University of South Africa

BOOK REVIEWS

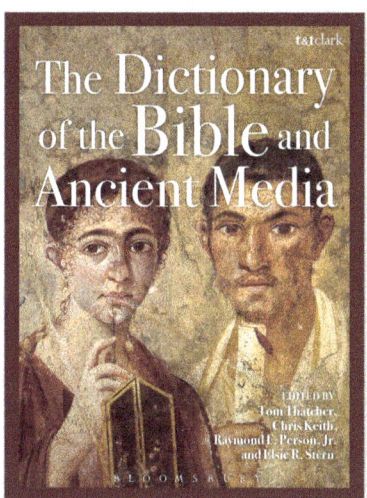

Tom Thatcher, Chris Keith, Raymond F. Person, Jr., and Elsie R. Stern, editors. *The Dictionary of the Bible and Ancient Media* (London: T&T Clark, 2017)

The *Dictionary of the Bible and Ancient Media* (*DBAM*) is an indispensable tool for students of biblical studies. Tom Thatcher writes that '*DBAM* strives to comprehend only the scope and distinct concerns of media criticism of the Bible, with emphasis on terms, themes and theories that might be encountered while reading a media-critical study' (p. xvii). And *DBAM* 'seeks to supplement, rather than replace, the existing library of biblical reference tools' (p. xvii). An excellent introduction by Raymond F. Person Jr. and Chris Keith ('Media Studies and Biblical Studies: An Introduction', pp.1–15) helpfully sets up the coherence of the entire dictionary.

Biblical studies are in a renaissance through dialogue with multiple fields, including comparative orality and sociology/psychology of memory. And the dialogue suggests significant implications for what were thought to be long established fundamentals. Much of the fresh momentum is the fruit of the 'Bible in Ancient and Modern Media Research Unit' of SBL, which helped to pioneer both performance criticism and social memory among other media advances (pp.36–40). Media perspectives 'continue to force scholars to reassess many assumptions about the creation, transmission, and circulation of traditions in early Christianity' (p.14). Pressure from these new avenues of inquiry is felt in, among other subjects, historical Jesus research and textual criticism. For example, textual criticism's focus on reconstructing the initial text is problematized by media's stress on 'the inherent pluriformity of the tradition', explaining that 'Jesus could have delivered the same sayings or sermons on multiple occasions' (p.415). The entry on 'Pluriformity' more forcibly maintains that 'it is not possible to speak of an original version but only of multiple performances' (pp.298–99).

Media dynamics also have implications for the Synoptic Problem—which still strongly favors a literary resolution. Newer findings suggest a much more complex interaction between orality and textuality in stated opposition to the 'Great Divide' paradigm which wrongly assumes that 'oral and written media are fundamentally different' (p.164). In contrast to the linear assessments of form criticism (see pp.142–46), media perspectives emphasize a dynamic context so that variations in the traditions are not necessarily the result of literary or editorial processes, but instead owe to different memories and oral performances, or the 're-oralisation' of written texts (p.363).

Though attention to the various media will no doubt shed light upon and provide lasting contributions for bible historians, the tendency to reduce singular and unrepeatable historical events to their subsequent reception and traditioning (pp.194–96, 196–98) may not be sufficiently dissimilar from form criticism and its appeal to *Sitze im Leben* (pp.11–14) so as to avoid the same fate. Historians in particular are interested in the events of the 'actual past' (p.18) just as much as their memory counterparts, however incomplete the inquiry and tentative the knowledge.

A significant majority of the *DBAM*

contributors are US researchers, but Germany, UK, Canada, Belgium, Israel, Sweden, and the Netherlands (pp.xi–xiii) are also represented. *DBAM* also provides entries on notable scholars such as Alan Dundes, Ruth Finnegan, John Miles Foley, Jack Goody, Marcel Jousse, Werner Kelber, Susan Niditch, and Walter Ong. Memory related entries proliferate, including: 'Cognitive/Personal Memory', 'Cold Memory/Hot Memory', 'Collective Memory/Social Memory', 'Communicative Memory', 'Countermemory', 'Cultural Memory', 'Flashbulb Memory', 'Gist Memory', 'Jesus Tradition and Memory', 'Personal Memory', 'Identity', 'Scribal Memory', 'Short-Term Memory', and 'Social Memory'. There is some confusion over 'Verbatim Memory'. In two places it is cited (pp.viii and 439) but there is no entry for it (see p.218). McIver's entry on 'Gist Memory' probably grew to encompass it (pp.156–57).

Certain jargon likely to prove unfamiliar for most researchers is also explained in independent entries, such as 'Biosphere (oral)', 'Chirograph', 'Register', or 'Sound Mapping'. Elements from linguistics are also furnished by *DBAM*, including 'Codeswitching', 'Sociolinguistics', and 'Discourse Analysis'. Additional and related entries such as 'Bilinguality' or 'Diglossia' would have been profitable.

Lastly, various literary corpora are provided with profitable insights from media studies. These include: 'Apocalypses, Early Christian', 'Apocalypses, Early Jewish', 'Dead Sea Scrolls and Other Judaean Desert Texts', 'Early Christian Literature', 'Early Jewish Literature', '1 Enoch/Enochic Traditions', 'Folklore/Folkloristics', 'Mishnah', 'Pauline Literature', 'Rabbinic Literature', and 'Wisdom Collections'.

The lasting significance of media approaches for biblical studies is difficult to estimate. On the one hand, it seems difficult to see the social tendencies apparent in media approaches displacing the classical approach to the Synoptic Problem or the canons of textual criticism for reconstructing the initial text. On the other hand, a great deal of influence has been seen and felt already. Besides *DBAM* itself, media's footprint can be seen in the journal *Oral Tradition* established by John Miles Foley (p.136), the Biblical Performance Criticism series by Cascade (Wipf & Stock), a host of monographs and dissertations, numerous essays involving memory in several New Testament journals such as *JSNT* and *JSHJ*, and the recent SBL groups BAMM and Mapping Memory.

Michael B. Metts
University of Aberdeen
Aberdeen, Scotland

BOOK REVIEWS

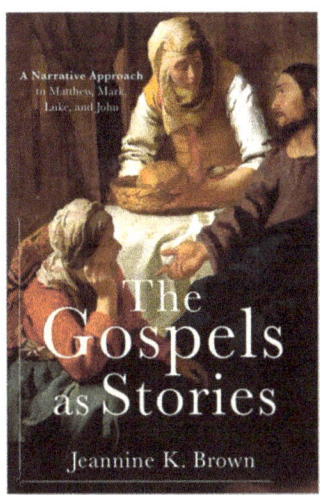

Jeannine Brown, *The Gospels as Stories: A Narrative Approach to Matthew, Mark, Luke and John* (Grand Rapids: Baker Academic, 2020)

Jeannine Brown has succeeded in writing an accessible book that unpacks some of the key elements of narrative criticism and applies them to the Gospel narratives. In her introduction, Brown gives a brief and accessible summary of the development of narrative criticism in Gospel studies, including ways in which it has adapted as a result of particular critiques. The remainder of the book is a series of alternating chapters: a methodological chapter outlining a key element of narrative criticism (plotting, characterisation, intertextuality, narrative theology) followed by a chapter that demonstrates the use of that element in a specific Gospel (Luke, Matthew, John and Mark respectively).

In her first methodological chapter, Brown explores the plotting activity of the Gospel writers, showing how their selection of material, together with its sequencing and pacing, create four distinctive interpretations of the same story. While examples are given from all Gospels, the literary theory of plotting is extensively demonstrated in Luke's Gospel showing how the structural elements of the Gospel point to the themes of discipleship and the inclusiveness of God's kingdom.

Brown then goes on to consider characterisation: how the Gospel writers portray the people in their stories. Here, Brown discusses the spectrum of flat to round characters, direct versus indirect characterisation and how the reliability (or otherwise) of characters is established. Brown makes a significant contribution to the topic of characterisation in biblical narrative by showing how characterisation can drive the plot forward and how characters can be used to embody themes. The following chapter shows how Matthew's characterisation of the disciples is used to shape the reader's journey of discipleship.

The next chapter covers intertextuality, building on Richard Hays' work of identifying scriptural echoes in the New Testament text. Brown unpacks the theory of stories evoking stories, showing how the Gospel writers use narrative patterns and characters from the Old Testament to illuminate the identity and mission of Jesus. This is ably demonstrated in the following chapter where Brown shows how intertextual echoes provide the foundation for John's Christology of Jesus as the Passover lamb, and John's portrayal of Jesus' ministry and resurrection as the renewal of creation.

In her final methodological chapter, Brown brings the previous elements together in order to show 'how a story theologizes'. One of the gems of this chapter is the rejection of the idea that narrative theology consists of 'a theological argument encased – or even imprisoned – in a narrative',[1] but rather allows for opposing tensions to be held together in a way that provokes deep engagement with the story. Thus, the reader should not be searching for the single overarching message in each Gospel. Instead, by paying close and sustained attention

---

1 Brown quotes Beverley Roberts Gaventa, 'Toward a Theology of Acts: Reading and Rereading', *Interpretation* 42 (1988), 146–57, here 149.

to the narrative and using the multiple lenses of plotting, characterisation and intertextuality, the reader will discover multiple themes and motifs as one would expect from a multifaceted story. In her final chapter, Brown demonstrates the theory of theologizing by looking at Mark's portrayal of God and the divine mission. This chapter was mildly disappointing. While the previous 'how-to' chapters were crystal clear in their application of theory, this one was, perhaps understandably, more abstract.

While Brown's work is firmly anchored in modern literary scholarship, she makes reference to ancient biographies and Greco-Roman rhetorical techniques, particularly in the methodological chapters on plotting and characterisation. In doing so, she demonstrates the validity of judiciously applying modern literary theory to ancient narratives. A helpful glossary, a list of recommended resources organised by chapter, a scripture index and subject index add to the user-friendliness of the book. Students and teachers of the Gospels will find this a practical book to have on their shelf.

Denise Powell
Malyon College

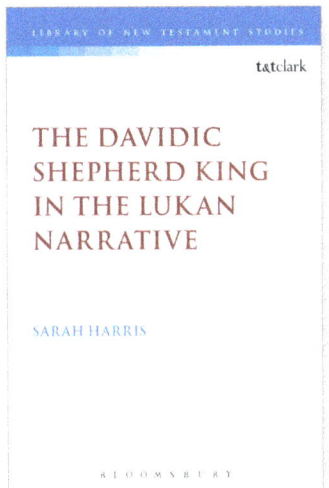

Sarah Harris, *The Davidic Shepherd King in the Lucan Narrative*
(LNTS 558. London, T & T Clark, 2016)

It is widely recognised that the fulfilment the messianic hope of Israel's scriptures was a major influence upon the Lucan corpus. Scholarship seeks to understand the nature of that influence by teasing out the threads which Luke has woven together in the composition of his Gospel and Acts. Sarah Harris' 2016 title, *The Davidic Shepherd King in the Lucan Narrative,* is an excellent contribution to this ongoing discussion. It is a fine example of intertextual research which seeks to establish the thesis that 'Luke's portrayal of Jesus as David is implicitly coloured by his nature as a shepherd king, which Luke demonstrates in explicit and implicit ways'. (p.1)

Harris acknowledges the influence of studies by François Bovon on Luke 15 and I. Howard Marshall on Luke 19:10, and notes how the Davidic theme in Luke-Acts has been studied in monographs by David Strauss (*The Davidic Messiah in Luke-Acts*, 1996) and Yuzuru Miura (*David in Luke-Acts: His Portrayal in the Light of Early Judaism,* 2007). However, she argues that there remains a lacuna in Lucan studies which she seeks to fill by studying Luke's presentation of Jesus as a specifically Davidic *shepherd* king, and by following this theme *beyond* its initial appearance in the birth and infancy narratives. Her study follows a narrative critical methodology and chapter 1 provides an excellent explanation of the aims and assumptions underlying this approach together with an analysis of scholars from a range of different fields who have contributed to the study of narrative method.

Then, in chapter 2, Harris describes the OT background to the Lucan motif by surveying the presentation of David in LXX 1 and 2 Kingdoms – focusing on the history of David's rise (1 Kingdoms 16 – 2 Kingdoms 5) and the Davidic covenant and beyond (2 Kingdoms 7, 12 and 24). From this she deduces: 'From David's earliest introduction to the final curtain call. He is a shepherd'. (p.19)

In this chapter Harris lays a solid foundation for her subsequent study of the Lucan material.

However, before considering the chapters which follow, two observations are in order. The first is a methodological point. The focus on the LXX text is valuable, and essential because of Luke's widely acknowledged reliance upon the Greek translation of Israel's scriptures, but this should not prevent Lucan scholars from keeping at least one eye on the MT. Might not Luke have been influenced by aspects of that account that are not reflected in the LXX? We will never know unless we look. A case in point is the difference between the MT and the LXX rendering of 2 Kingdoms 12:6. The MT has David respond to Nathan's parable of the callous rich man by insisting that he restore the lamb *fourfold,* yet in the LXX David makes a more extreme demand—*sevenfold* restoration. Harris offers helpful comments on the LXX presentation, but does not consider the divergence from the MT. Might this not warrant further investigation in view of the *fourfold* restoration offered by Zacchaeus in

Luke 19:8, a verse which figures prominently in chapter 5?

A second observation is that Harris's subsequent study of the Davidic shepherd king in Luke draws not only on the historical narrative of 1 and 2 Kingdoms, but also the prophetic development of the Davidic theme in Isaiah and Micah, and most clearly in Ezekiel 34. In view of the subsequent emphasis on these passages, it would have been helpful to have included them in the foundational survey of chapter 2.

The main body of the study is found in chapters 3–5 where Harris traces the Davidic shepherd king through the birth and infancy narratives (chapter 3); the travel narrative (chapter 4); and account of Jesus' encounter with Zacchaeus (chapter 5). Chapter 3 surveys the six direct references to David in Luke 1–2 (1:27; 1:28–38; 1:46–55; 1:68–79; 2:4, 11; and 2:41–52); and includes a substantial study of the significance of the shepherds in Luke 2:8–20, which concludes by approving Bovon's assessment that the shepherds set the scene for presenting Jesus as the messianic shepherd (p.67). Chapter 4 begins by linking the household mission (10:3), Jesus' saying in Luke 12:32, the parable of the faithful shepherd (15:1–9); and Paul's exhortation to the Ephesian elders (Acts 20:28–29) to the Davidic shepherd theme.

Chapter 5 provides a detailed study of Jesus' encounter with Zacchaeus (19:1–10), which is found at the end of the travel narrative as Jesus' ministry outside Jerusalem comes to an end. Following her narrative critical method Harris presents this passage as a summary statement which builds on an intratextual platform established in a succession of passages which establish the presentation of Jesus as the faithful shepherd who comes to seek the salvation of the lost. In this way Jesus fulfils the mission he described in his Nazareth sermon (4:18–19). 'In many ways the two sayings make the same point, while the second defines how that ministry is carried out. It is carried out as God's faithful shepherd'. (p.148) In order to sustain this thesis Harris carefully summarises and rejects the argument that Luke 19:1–10 is a vindication rather than a salvation narrative.

Throughout this monograph Harris' work is characterised by thorough and insightful exegesis as well as respectful but rigorous interaction with alternate views. In the concluding chapter she makes several helpful suggestions for ongoing research. These include the significance of Ezekiel 34 in Luke's presentation of Jesus' ministry; the place of the house as a 'sacred space' for ministry in place of the Jerusalem temple; a re-reading of Luke's use of Isaiah 53 with the sheep motif in view; and an examination of the self-understanding of the historical Jesus in relation to the Davidic shepherd motif. This monograph lays strong foundations upon which such research may build.

Andrew Stewart
Reformed Theological College, Melbourne

BOOK REVIEWS

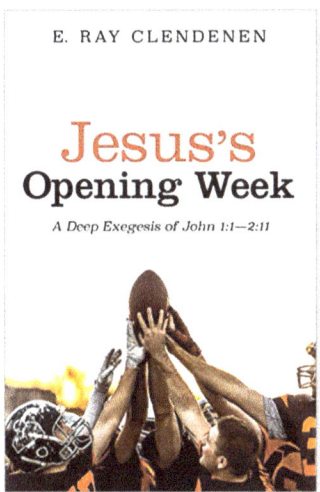

E. Ray Clendenen, *Jesus' Opening Week: A Deep Exegesis of John 1:1–2:11*
(Eugene: Wipf & Stock, 2019)

E. Ray Clendenen is senior editor of Bibles and reference books for Lifeway Christian Resources in Nashville. A former professor of Hebrew and Old Testament, he is the general editor of the New American Commentary and author of the volume on Malachi. Besides editing several other Bible reference works, he is the author of over fifty book chapters and articles on the Bible, theology, and Bible translation. He is also a leader in the Celebrate Recovery ministry. Clendenen has also been an obituary writer (1974–75), and outboard motor mechanic (1967–73), and studied anthropology at Rice University before pursuing ministry. I list the latter as additional notes on his published biography to paint the picture of a man who has seen more than the inside of a lecture theatre and writes for more than just academics. Clendenen has personally been helped out of darkness by God, people and the truth of God's word, and the Spirit. This led him to a newfound interest in the Christian union with Christ, Paul's letter to the church at Galatia and John's Gospel. This interest drives the present work which is both theologically rich and immensely practical, commended for a wide readership but especially tailored towards 'those who are called to minister the gospel of Christ to a hurting world'.[1] Since one strength of this book is it's concise nature, an additional commendation might be for those called to minister the gospel *who find themselves time-poor*.

The book is broken into three major sections with an introduction and conclusion nicely topping and tailing the work. The three central chapters are rich in expository work, moving through John 1–2:11 in a well ordered, detailed, yet efficient manner. For the most part, the internal structure of the chapters is divided into the days of Jesus' opening week.

This contribution is one of the most thoroughly researched exegetical companions I have read. It does not go 'into the weeds' in the same manner as a commentary, yet leaves traces of working to allow the source material to be easily found. Reading it is reminiscent of sitting in a theological college study room and having one mate who has simply done all the work, read all the books, and can somehow talk you through it in a way where you don't feel like an idiot. Instead, you find yourself reading John's Gospel afresh wondering why you didn't see things earlier.

While working exegetically through the opening week, Clendenen interjects with personal anecdotes and application that are often hugely beneficial. At times I felt that some of these could have been flagged a little more clearly, for the structure of the argument becomes somewhat muddied before the work on the text resumes. Perhaps it is a personal preference, but a greater internal structure to the chapters would have aided the work.

---

1 Clendenen, *Jesus' Opening Week: A Deep Exegesis of John 1:1–2:11* (Eugene: Wipf and Stock, 2019), p. xii

BOOK REVIEWS

Areas of thought provoked

Two interesting areas of thought were provoked for me as a result of reading Clendenen's work. Firstly, the concept of Jesus 'Opening Week' is touched on in the preface and lightly treated throughout the book itself. Clendenen notes in the preface the power of this idea if explored properly:

> this Opening section of John's Gospel helps tie together the whole Bible, reading back to the week of creation and ahead to the week of new-creation fulfilment in Jesus's climatic passion week'.[2]

This idea is anchored in Bauckham's compelling argument laid out in *Gospel of Glory*. This idea, however, could have been expanded on in greater depth. I have not much to offer to aid with that depth, but Clendenen's work certainly has inspired me to look in greater detail at the opening week of Jesus in John 1–2 and its potential symmetry with his passion week.

Secondly, Keener's recent work (published after *Jesus' Opening Week*) *Christobiography* offers an exciting new level of detail into the writing of the Gospels and situates them well among the first-century biographical literature. It would be fascinating to hear Clendenen continue his work in this piece with a further look at how the potential opening week structure fits within the early biographical habits of the time. Keener notes that:

> if Luke falls on the more historiographic end of biography, John seems to embrace he genres flexibility more fully, perhaps more encomiastically'.[3]

The 'flexibility' that Keener notes, I believe is what Clendenen has picked up on in his contribution. Further analysis of early examples of similar biographical flair may aid the church in understanding the structure of John's Gospel better and its contribution to the Bible as a whole.

A warm contribution

Clendenen, though, prioritised the mission of reminding the children of Christ that God is love. He wants the preacher in the pulpit to not only know and love Christ but be passionately stirred to know and love him better. This encouragement is not dissimilar to being fired up by a coach of a sports team, but it feels much like a warm embrace. The conversation partners that Clendenen brings in are not purely academic but are also from the arts. Therefore, this contribution does a terrific job at probing both mind and heart. He ministers to those in a hurting world and offers the solution—grace.

Chris Booth
Chaplain, Australian Defence Force
Townsville

---

2   Clendenen, *Jesus' Opening Week*, p. 10

3   Keener, *Christobiography: Memory, History, and the Reliability of the Gospels* (Grand Rapids: Eerdmans, 2019), p.347-8

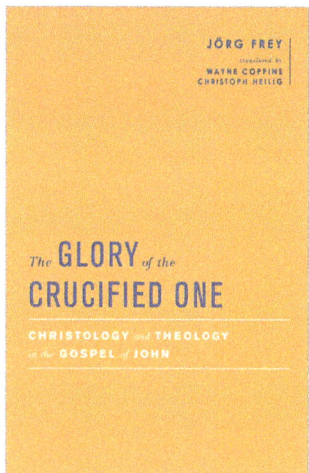

Jörg Frey, *The Glory of the Crucified One: Christology and Theology in the Gospel of John*. (Waco, TX: Baylor University Press, 2018)

This collection of essays from Jörg Frey presents in English a broad spectrum of his works. In some ways this is the translation of an earlier German language collection, although there are notable differences in the content. It makes accessible in English the work of one of the leading active Johannine scholars. Much of the work within forms a foundation for his forthcoming EKKNT commentary. The volume begins with some personal reflections, the story of a scholar. Frey studied under Martin Hengel at Tübingen, and it was Hengel who led Frey into his early research into Johannine eschatology. Frey characterises his approach as reflecting a focus on the backgrounds of the text, especially working with the Qumran texts. He also highlights a need to attend to the theological claims of the text alongside questions of history.

The first essay is methodological, setting out the main scholarly approaches to the Gospel before Frey locates his own work in context. Unsurprisingly, Frey interacts with mostly other German scholars, although key English-language sources are usually present. Frey begins with theological approaches, which seek to extract Christological and soteriological truths from the narrative, of which Bultmann is the paradigmatic example (Bultmann and Käsemann often appear throughout the volume as examples of alternate poles of interpretation, with Frey consistently avoiding either extreme). This is contrasted with those who focus on the Gospel as a history of the earthly Jesus, a perspective of which Frey is critical—such as Anderson's work to retrieve John as a source for the historical Jesus. A third approach Frey calls the contemporary-historical approach, which uses the Gospel as evidence for the situation of the composition of the Gospel, with Martyn and Wengst as notable examples. Frey argues that there is a fusion of horizons between the time of Jesus and that of the author and addressees. Yet he also questions whether conflict with the Jews is truly the defining framework for the Gospel.

Frey then turns to source and redaction critical approaches to the Gospel, of which he is broadly critical. He does not reject the idea of earlier sources, but rather sees those earlier sources as no longer recoverable. Finally, Frey turns to literary or narrative approaches. These Frey see as important, yet equally he critiques them for overly bracketing out historical or source questions, especially when historical assumptions still shape interpretations. Thus, Frey argues that all the traditional approaches have limits, and they need to be used together. He characterises his approach as a narrative focus that is sceptical of source criticism, but sees as valid questions around author, audience, historical and religious contexts, and at least the question of sources, even if those questions are not answerable. The combination of narrative and critical concerns sees Frey take a broadly similar approach to someone like Frank Moloney, albeit more shaped by the German-speaking tradition.

Part two of the book tackles broad questions of the character of the Gospel. It begins with a study on 'the Jews' in John. Frey's contribution here is to argue for a dramaturgical function to the term, noting its distribution through the text and links to 'the world'. He argues that at the time of writing, the context was one of inner-community schism rather than conflict with the Jews. Where there was conflict with the Jews, Frey sees it as resulting from a post-70 CE context where the *fiscus judaicus* raises the stakes for the question 'who is a Jew?'. He argues that this tax was a substantial motivator for the separation of Jews and Christians and provides a connection between conflict with the Jews and conflict with the world.

The next chapter addresses the temporal framework of the Gospel, with Frey arguing that John represents a 'fusion of temporal horizons', drawing on Gadamer. He sees the Gospel bringing together the time of the earthly Jesus and that of the post-Easter community. Unlike Martyn, Frey does not see these two temporal perspectives as separable within the Johannine narrative, but they are intertwined as the later interpretation of Jesus is pushed back into the earlier events. The function of the fusion of horizons is to enable the audience to understand its situation and challenges anew.

> John's concern is ... with the implications of post-Easter faith in the risen crucified and incarnate one.

The final chapter in the first part deals with dualism in John. Frey rejects any direct history of religions explanation for the dualism in John, arguing that even the dualism of Qumran is too varied to provide a coherent background for John. Instead, dualistic motifs serve a dramaturgical function, but are subordinated to, and are used to convey, Christology. As such, some dualities are asymmetric, so the positive aspects of light or life are developed more extensively than their negatives. Nor do the dualisms reflect a fixed world-community boundary, but the opposition of the world is presented in the context of a renewed turning to the world rather than a retreat from it.

The third part of the book focuses on 'the hour', which for Frey has central interpretative significance. Within this section the first chapter is an exploration of the ways in which Jesus' death has been understood. Jesus' death fits many aspects of ancient ideas of the honourable or heroic death, although for John it is more than an outward showing of honour. It is an effective death in that it achieves something, although the presentation demands more of a theological explanation. Jesus death is vicarious, seen not only through language of 'on behalf of', but also through narratives where there is an exchange of places. Frey also sees merit in understanding Jesus' death as atoning, for while the explicit language is not present, Jesus' death is presented as sin-removing and life-enabling. Frey concludes that no single motif sufficiently expresses Jesus' death as conveyed in John.

The next chapter explores the idea of bodiliness, not in terms of asserting historicity but highlighting the way that for John the real space-time dimensions of the story matter. There are concrete places and times, along with physical details of emotion and suffering. The senses all play a role within the narrative. The bodiliness climaxes in eschatological terms with bodily resurrection. This is seen especially with the account of Lazarus, where his resurrection is clearly depicted in a bodily fashion, while linking it closely to Jesus' own resurrection. Yet in Jesus' resurrection appearances, when compared to Luke there is less emphasis on Jesus being corporeal. Thus, Frey argues, John's concern is not primarily anti-docetic, but with the implications of post-Easter faith in the risen crucified and incarnate one.

The third part culminates with a chapter that bears the same title as the book itself. 'The Glory of the Crucified One' focuses on the relationship between the δόξα of the earthly Jesus and the δόξα of the preincarnate one. He argues the Farewell Discourse and the motif of the 'hour' are key. Jesus' glory is only seen when recognising the glorification of the crucified one, and thus is only visible post-Easter.

The fourth part of the book turns to Christology and theology, beginning with incarnation. Taking John 1:14 as the focus, Frey focuses on the uses of σκηνόω as explaining 'the word became flesh'. Thus, the Jewish background is significant, and interprets the incarnation in relation to Shekinah theology. The incarnation is neither merely taking on humanity like a piece of clothing, nor is it an abandonment of divinity, but it is God dwelling with his people. While making a reasonable argument, this chapter was one of the weaker chapters in that it did not seem to present significantly new ideas.

Frey then turns to the idea of Jesus as the image of God. The uniqueness of the Johannine picture is found in the idea of Jesus as the exclusive image of God. Jesus presents God in terms of his divine identity, seen in the signs as well as the discourses. The reciprocal immanence of the Father and Son bring this beyond functioning as representation to be presentation. God's nature is now disclosed in Jesus.

After this focus on Christology, Frey turns to theology proper, as in how the Gospel depicts God himself. As the previous chapter indicated, Jesus reveals God himself, and thus Christology and theology are intimately linked. Presenting Jesus as divine reshapes the picture of God. Frey sees God pictured both in the narrative, but especially in the predicates of spirit, and in 1 John of light and love. Thus, Frey argues that according to John, God is not hidden but revealed, has entered into history and revealed his love definitively at the cross, enabled unrestricted worship through the spirit, and in this reflects proto-trinitarian ideas.

The final chapter presents the idea of John as the climax of New Testament theology. By this, Frey carefully sets out that he does not mean that John has the most developed theology in all areas, but that in many, especially key areas of the Christology and the doctrine of God, John goes beyond earlier writings. Seeing John as one of the later documents in the NT, Frey identifies a more developed Christology—not that John was the first to have a high Christology, but that the idea of Jesus as θεός is conveyed in a more considered manner. As in the previous chapter, the oneness of Father and Son leads to a more developed doctrine of God. To this is added the talk of the Spirit as paraclete, and thus personal, which along with depicting the spirit as the gift of Jesus not just of God, evinces proto-Trinitarian ideas. Finally, Frey sees the hermeneutical perspective of John as more developed, canonising not only the words of Jesus (as in the other Gospels) but also later theological insights.

The essays that comprise this collection have been carefully chosen to present a breadth of Frey's scholarship, touching on many of the key interpretative issues in the Gospel of John. There is a coherence to the collection as the interpretative method set out in the first chapter is consistently applied throughout. Additionally, there are clear links between the topics covered, and the interpretations offered are mutually coherent. The breadth of this collection mean that this book will be of interest and use to any involved in Johannine studies. It offers a helpful window into German scholarship for an English-speaking context, as well as providing many further references for those that wish to explore that German scholarship further. This work is the fruit of decades of working on John, and they show clarity, nuance, and a balanced judgement of many earlier arguments. It is easy to see this book becoming an essential resource for all those working in the Gospel of John.

Chris Seglenieks
Bible College of South Australia

BOOK REVIEWS

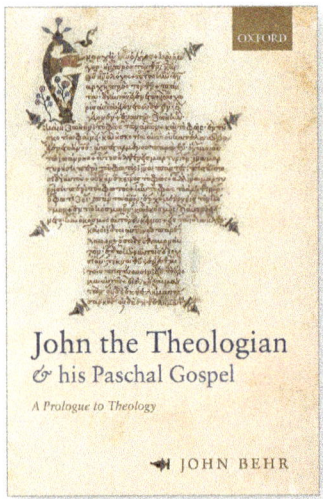

Behr, John. *John the Theologian and his Paschal Gospel: A Prologue to Theology* (Oxford: OUP, 2019)

John Behr has written a provocative book on John that seeks to argue for a radically different reading of the Gospel. Central to the book is his contention that the incarnation is not a past event but is 'the ongoing embodiment of God in those who follow Christ' (viii). It is not a commentary, although at times there is a detailed focus on specific passages, notably John 6 and the Prologue. As might be expected from Behr, his work is heavily shaped by patristic readings, but alongside historical and exegetical investigations, are added philosophical reflections from phenomenology.

First, Behr sets out some methodological concerns that will shape what follows. He warns against what he sees as a key problem, which is that John is read with the doctrine of incarnation as understood today as a framing concept. Behr rejects the idea that the author or early audience of the Gospel had any concept of the pre-incarnate Word being born in flesh as 'an episode in the biography of the Word', using Rowan Williams' words that appear repeatedly throughout the book. Behr attacks the traditional reading of the incarnation by raising the problem of ascribing temporality to a divine subject. Rather, taking a cue from writers such as Athanasius, 'Word' should be understood as a title ascribed to Jesus, and the Cross, rather than pre-existence, as the focal point for understanding the incarnation.

The book engages with three sets of readers of John. First are the early fathers, particularly those that Behr identifies as part of a 'school' of John: Polycarp, Papias, Melito, Apollinaris, Polycrates, and Irenaeus. Second are modern biblical scholars, while third is a singular reader, the French phenomonologist Michel Henry. The inclusion of other readers beyond modern biblical scholars is a good shake up for those of us who are used to more limited readings of John, challenging the assumption that our paradigm is necessarily correct. However, the more metaphysical discussions may take some getting used to for those without a philosophical background.

The work falls into three parts. The first establishes some interpretative parameters. The patristic sources form the basis for Behr's argument that John the Elder (not John the son of Zebedee) is the author of the Gospel. By exploring the Johannine 'school' and their connection to the Quartodeciman controversy, Behr argues that this John is the high priest of the Pascha, and his Gospel is a paschal gospel. Behr also advocates common authorship with Revelation, a connection that becomes significant as he reads John as an apocalyptic gospel. The idea of John as an apocalyptic Gospel is developed in dialogue with modern scholarship, particularly that of Käsemann, Martyn, and most prominently Ashton. Behr characterises the Gospel as a counterpart to Revelation, where what is revealed in Revelation is in the Gospel veiled in narrative.

The second part of the book is more exegetical in character, beginning with a chapter exploring the Temple theme. Through this chapter Behr largely follows the work of Coloe and to a lesser extent Leithart. Within this chapter Behr addresses John 6, which he argues is not focused on the reality of the incarnation versus Docetism, nor is it sacramental. Rather the ascent (John 6:62) is what enables the descent of the life-giving flesh and blood. However, the argument is oversimplified as Behr presents the only alternative to his view as one that is effectively endorsing cannibalism. This overlooks alternative positions, such as the image of eating and drinking being a metaphor for believing, as Maarten Menken argues.

Continuing on, the Passion in John is understood as a unity of cross, resurrection and return to the Father. In this light, the Passion is the raising of a new Temple, with a new sacrifice and a new priest. However, the presence of John beside the cross includes him within the priestly role, while Jesus' words from the cross are understood to create a new household of God. Then the Revelation image of the marriage of Christ and the Church is taken as the means by which God has his dwelling with humans. This Behr links back to John 1:14, arguing that it is by eating the ascended flesh of Christ that Christ tabernacles in us.

The second chapter investigates the idea of being a 'living human being'. Behr draws connections with the opening chapters of Genesis to argue that the Cross is the completion of God's work of making a human in his image. While arguing that the ascending and descending motif in John is not about birth and return to the Father, Behr downplays some of the evidence that supports the traditional reading, such as the descending Holy Spirit (1:32–34) and the ascending Jesus (20:17) which suggest the life of Jesus is framed by ascent and descent. Neither does Behr interact with the arguments against allowing Genesis 28 to control the interpretation of John 1:51 as made by Loader and van der Watt. While the Johannine ascent-descent motif and the associated Son of Man title are complex, the narrow focus leaves Behr's argument wanting at this point.

The third and final chapter in this part examines the Prologue. Here Behr returns to the objection to speaking of the Word as having a 'story' before the birth of Jesus. While undoubtedly some understandings of the incarnation may be problematic when considered in light of traditional doctrines of God, Behr blurs the distinction between such problematic conceptions and all other traditional readings of the Johannine Prologue. Behr rejects the idea that 'the Word became flesh' in John 1:14 refers to Jesus' birth as a human. Instead, Behr reinterprets the prologue in light of his reinterpretation of John 6. As he argues that John 6 presents the need for Jesus to ascend before he can distribute his body as the bread of life to be consumed, thus in 1:14 the 'becoming flesh' is about Jesus' ascension that enables his body to be received as flesh that gives life. This connects to understanding the Prologue as a paschal hymn, and thus in Behr's reading the focus is upon the cross rather than the birth of Jesus. Behr then follows this up with the claim that 1:12–13 and 1:14 are 'obviously' references to baptism and the Eucharist (p.267)—a case where what is obvious to one person is far from it for others.

Through these exegetical sections, Behr assumes that details such as shifts in tense and sayings such as 'the hour is coming and now is' indicate a conflation of the events of Jesus' life and the present reality of the community. This is implicitly significant for the overall argument, as the reading presented effectively assumes an audience who are attuned to a certain way of reading the Gospel, who know when coming to the Prologue that becoming flesh must be read in light of later passages. A wider audience would undermine this reading—for example, a Greek reader not already shaped by this reading might easily assume that 'the Word became flesh' refers to a divine principle becoming embodied.

> **The Passion in John is understood as a unity of cross, resurrection and return to the Father,**

The final part of the book turns to the work of Michel Henry, who has written on phenomenology in light of John's Gospel. His concern is with how things manifest, and distinctions between the reality of something and the way in which it appears in the world. In his framework, Christ is pure manifestation, with echoes of Bultmann evident as he says Christ reveals not something else but himself. There is a focus on 'living' as something that cannot be observed but only experienced, and that flesh is what God has vivified. For Henry, it is not Scripture itself that reveals Truth, for only Truth can reveal itself. Behr does not go so far, but rather sees the Passion as what unveils the Scriptures, calling us back to an identity already established in the life and suffering of Christ which precedes and embraces our suffering and life.

> The Passion as what unveils the Scriptures.

Behr concludes with this summary: John is the high priest of the paschal mystery; the Gospel is a paschal gospel and the Prologue is a paschal hymn. By lifting Christ up on the cross, the world is placed in judgement, as the veil is lifted from Scripture, revealing the building of the temple and the completion of God's project to make a human being in his image. The conclusion then outlines the implications that Behr sees that his rereading of John has for the task of theology. He argues that the Passion must be the starting point for theological reflection. The starting point for understanding Christ, however, is the Old Testament as unveiled by the cross, rather than the New Testament. In the Passion, Christ shows both what it is to be God and what it is to be human.

Overall, this book is a challenging and stimulating read. By expanding the circle of interlocutors Behr proposes new (or at times very old but forgotten) readings. As such, this is a valuable resource for those who want to grapple with the Gospel on different terms, rather than merely assuming the parameters of modern biblical scholarship. However, Behr does not marshal sufficient evidence to necessitate overturning prior readings of John. Therefore, we are left with a plausible patristic reading of John, one that will certainly provoke thoughts and discussions, but one which may not ultimately be persuasive.

Chris Seglenieks
Bible College of South Australia

BOOK REVIEWS

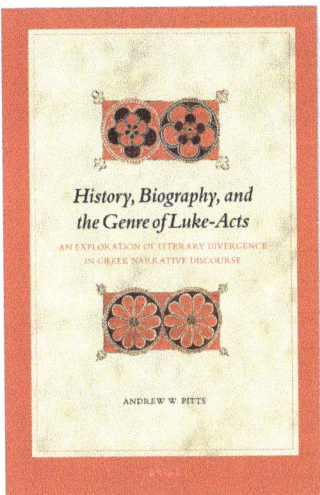

Andrew W. Pitts. *History, Biography, and the Genre of Luke-Acts: An Exploration of Literary Divergence in Greek Narrative Discourse* (Leiden and Boston: Brill, 2019)

The identification of the genre of the Gospels as βίος, or biography, is commonplace. The question of how Acts, as the second part in Luke's two-part work Luke-Acts, relates to this generic categorisation is less straightforward. In *History, Biography, and the Genre of Luke-Acts*, Andrew W. Pitts makes a valuable contribution to the ongoing discussion regarding the genre of Luke-Acts.

Pitts begins by acknowledging the dominant place of Richard Burridge's monograph *What are the Gospels?* in the scholarly identification of the Gospels as biography (pp.3–10). His critique, however, is that while Burridge identifies the Gospels as biography on the basis of generic similarities, he does not consider elements of generic divergence. Pitts' volume proposes a model of genre analysis that considers both generic similarities and divergences in order to identify Luke-Acts genre.

Pitts uses Systemic Functional Linguistics as the methodological foundation for his study. He explains: 'The *systemic element* of SFL should not be confused with *systematic*. The term is used to signify that the fundamental concept in language is that of system. What is a system? An SFL system is nothing more than a set of linguistic options, classified typologically by opposing relations' (p.20). Drawing on the work of J.R. Martin and David Rose (pp.18–27), Pitts argues that Luke-Acts can be analysed in terms of eight 'clines' or scales—with history and βίος at opposing ends—along which one might locate features of the narrative in order to identify its genre agnation, ie. its similarity to or divergence from a particular genre (pp.40–43).

The clines which Pitts adopts for his analysis of Luke-Acts are as follows. The first two are broader categories: 1. Topical focus, in which history is activity focused and βίοι are entity focused; and 2. Participant identification, in which history tends to focus on generic participants (ie. groups), and βίοι on individual participants. The next four are frames, which are 'macro-level structures that help "frame" or stage the narrative' (p.42). These are: 3. Initiation, panoramic in history and focalised in βίοι; 4. Commencement, which is event-driven in history and participant-driven in βίοι; 5. Self-identification, which is nonbiographical in history and biographical in βίοι; and 6. Genealogies, which are embedded in history and staged in βίοι. The final two clines are: 7. Time management, which is episodic in history while βίοι tend towards 'field time', 'the gradual unfolding of time from the perspective of ... the subject of the βίος' (p.42); and 8. Authentication strategies, which are 'bounded' in history and 'unbounded' in βίοι. This final cline refers to the densities of citations of sources—lower in history and higher in βίοι.

After identifying a representative corpus of Greek histories and βίοι against which to compare Luke-Acts (ch. 2), chapters 3 to 6 comprise of Pitts' analysis of Luke-Acts and comparative literature in terms of the eight clines. Regarding the first cline—Focus—Pitts notes that Greek histories focus on activities whereas βίοι focus on entities, particularly the individual who is the subject of the βίος. Comparing Luke to the other Gospels, he notes that Matthew, Mark and John all clearly introduce Jesus as the subject in the first verses of the first chapter (p.80). Luke, on the other hand, does not mention Jesus in his prologue, but rather 'composes a narrative of activities accomplished among "us" based on eyewitness testimony of these *events*' (p.79, emphasis original). Luke also moves away from biographical interests by delaying Jesus' birth narrative and placing his death and resurrection in the centre of the two-part work (p.79).

Pitts' claim that the activity- (rather than entity-) focused nature of the prologue to Luke's Gospel locates it within the genre of history raised the question in my mind of what to make of Luke's recapitulation in Acts 1. There Luke notes that in his first work he had recorded what 'Jesus began to do and to teach' (Acts 1:1), seemingly identifying the Gospel as a βίος. This question is answered in Pitts' discussion of cline 3—Initiations—in chapter 4. He argues that in multi-volume historical works, book-level transitions 'often recruit anaphoric individualized participant identification strategies' (p.107). That is, a recapitulation of an individual's words and deeds commonly appeared in book-level initiations in Greek histories.

Pitts' analysis of Luke-Acts in relation to the rest of the clines produces similar results. Luke-Acts, especially when considered together as a multivolume work, consistently agnates closer to Greek histories than βίοι. The author's argument is well developed, and I think convincing. The strength of Pitts' approach is that it offers a way forward to identify the genre of Luke-Acts as a unified work, rather than forcing Luke into the biographical genre and leaving Acts floating on the sidelines.

David A. Evans
Macquarie University, Sydney

www.ingramcontent.com/pod-product-compliance
Lightning Source LLC
Chambersburg PA
CBHW051255110526
44588CB00026B/3002